The Syntax Workbook

For my family: Jean, Fiona, Morag, and Pangur

The Syntax Workbook

A Companion to Carnie's Syntax

Andrew Carnie

WILEY-BLACKWELL

A John Wiley & Sons, Inc., Publication

Contents

Introduction

Welcome

Thank you for purchasing *The Syntax Workbook* which goes along with the third edition of *Syntax: A Generative Introduction*. This workbook is designed to give you further practice beyond the presentation and exercises in the main text. Syntax often uses big tree diagrams, and the constant cry I've heard from students using the first and second editions is that there aren't enough example diagrams or practice. On the other hand, adding practice exercises with answers would make the main text too big and expensive. So I've settled on this optional workbook as an alternative.

You have three different opportunities to practice now:

1) *Workbook Exercises (WBE)*: This workbook contains enrichment and additional practice exercises that go along with each chapter in the book. You can check your own answers against the answer key at the end of each chapter.

2) *General Problem Sets (GPS) (in the main textbook)*: You can do the general problem sets at the end of each chapter in the main textbook. I'm sorry but *the answers to these questions are not made available to students*. The reason for this is that many instructors use these problem sets as a means for student evaluation. Providing the answers to these would be counterproductive! If you are using the textbook for self-study or your

The Syntax Workbook, First Edition. Andrew Carnie.
© 2013 Andrew Carnie. Published 2013 by John Wiley & Sons, Inc.

instructor isn't using the problem sets for evaluation, I encourage you to find a linguistics professor or linguistics (post-)graduate student who can help you with determining if you are on the right track with these.

3)   If you are an advanced student or a graduate student, I strongly encourage you to try the ***Challenge Problem Sets (CPS)*** at the end of each chapter in the main textbook. These problem sets are designed to make you think critically about the presentation in the text and to think about alternatives and problems that exist for the theory. Again the answers to these cannot be distributed to students.

I hope that you find that the addition of this workbook enriches your syntactic studies and gives you more opportunities to master the material.

This is the first version of this workbook and while we've done our best at quality control, it's possible that some errors have slipped through the student testing, copy-editing, and proofreading processes. I welcome any corrections or suggestions at carnie@email.arizona. edu. You should check my website or the Wiley-Blackwell website listed below to see if there are any errata available for this workbook or for the main text.

Many people have contributed to the creation and production of this book. My thanks to: Dean Allemagn, Diana Archangeli, Glynis Baguley, Uldis Balodis, Andrew Barss, Jean Carnie, Fiona Carnie, Morag Carnie, Pangur Carnie, Jae Hoon Choi, Danielle Descoteaux, Charlotte Frost, Carrie Gillon, Andrea Haber, Heidi Harley, Mike Hammond, Hyun Kyoung Jung, Dan Karvonen, Simin Karimi, Julia Kirk, Jeff Lidz, Dave Medeiros, Leah Morin, Alan Munn, Diane Ohala, Matt Pearson, David Pesetsky, Massimo Piatelli-Palmarini, Colin Phillips, Bill Poser, Jeff Punske, Marlita Reddy-Hjelmfelt, Sylvia Reed, Bob Ritchie, Jeff Runner, Yosuke Sato, Kevin Schluter, Dan Siddiqi, Peter Slomanson, Megan Stone, Maggie Tallerman, Chris Tancredi, Deniz Tat, Alex Trueman, Sakari Vaelma, the students in my various LING300 Syntax Classes at the University of Arizona, and my Facebook friends who I regularly victimized as testers for the problem sets in the book. I'm sure I've forgotten someone here, but please know you're appreciated anyway.

Andrew Carnie
Tucson

http://dingo.sbs.arizona.edu/~carnie
http://www.wiley.com/go/carnie

chapter 1

Generative Grammar

WORKBOOK EXERCISES

WBE1.   PRESCRIPTIVE RULES
[Critical Thinking; Basic]

Part 1: All of the sentences below are prescriptively "wrong" according to many language mavens. Can you identify what's supposed to be wrong with them (i.e. what prescriptive rule do they violate?). If you're not familiar with prescriptive rules you may have to search around on the Web a bit to figure this out, but if you've been trained to write in the American or British University tradition, most (or many) of these should stand out as "poor grammar" or "poor style". Certainly, Microsoft Word's grammar-checking program is flagging each of these sentences as I write them!

a) What did you put the present in?
b) She's smarter than him.
c) To boldly go where no one has gone before!
d) He walks too slow.
e) Hopefully, the weather will turn sunny soon.
f) I found out something which will disturb you greatly.
g) Who did you see?

The Syntax Workbook, First Edition. Andrew Carnie.
© 2013 Andrew Carnie. Published 2013 by John Wiley & Sons, Inc.

h)   I can't hardly sleep.
i)   10 items or less [a grocery store sign]
j)   My view of grammar is different than yours.
k)   I will not enjoy it.
l)   If I was a linguist, then I wouldn't have to study prescriptive rules.
m)   The homework wasn't done completely.
n)   All of the linguists at the conference congratulated each other.
o)   Me and John are going to the movies later.
p)   I want to learn a new language like French.

Part 2: Consider each of the sentences above and evaluate whether or not they are really unacceptable for you. Try to ignore what you were taught in school was right, and focus instead on whether you might actually utter one of these sentences, or if you'd actually blink if you heard one of them produced by someone else. Listen to your inner voice rather than relying on what you have learned is "correct".

WBE2.   SCIENTIFIC METHOD PRACTICE[1]
[Critical Thinking Practice; Basic]

Background: One particular kind of question in English is called a "*Yes/No* question". These questions can typically be answered with either *Yes, No,* or *Maybe.* The standard strategy for forming *Yes/No* questions is to change the order of the words at the beginning of the sentence from the equivalent statement:

a)   John hasn't eaten anything.   *Statement*
b)   Hasn't John eaten anything?   Yes/No *question*

With this background about *yes/no* and declarative sentences in mind, consider the following hypothesis:

> *Hypothesis 1*: Yes/No *questions are formed by moving the second word in the equivalent statement to the front.*

Now look at the follow sentences:

c)   Bilbo will eat chocolate-covered sausage.   *Statement*
d)   Will Bilbo eat chocolate-covered sausage?   Yes/No *question*

Question 1: Are sentences (c) and (d) consistent with hypothesis 1? (Pay careful attention to the wording of the hypothesis!)
    Now consider the next two sentences

e)   The old hobbit will eat the chocolate-covered sausage.   *Statement*
f)   Will the old hobbit eat the chocolate-covered sausage?   Yes/No *question*

---

[1]   Loosely based on an exercise in Carnie (2011).

Question 2: Are sentences (e) and (f) consistent with hypothesis 1?

Question 3: Instead of (f), what sentence does hypothesis 1 actually predict to be the grammatical *Yes/No* question equivalent to (e)?

Question 4: Try to come up with a hypothesis that accounts for the grammaticality of (e). (Hint #1: words such as *will* are called **auxiliaries**. Hint #2: use as much of the language in hypothesis 1 as you can, making only minimal changes.)

WBE3. USING CORPORA FOR DOING SYNTACTIC RESEARCH
[Critical Thinking Practice; Basic]

Make sure you read the discussion of *blow up* in section 3.2 of chapter 1 before attempting this question. Consider the phrase "blow off". In colloquial American English, this sequence has two[2] usages with quite different meanings.

a) The leaves blew off the sidewalk.
b) I blew off doing my homework.

In (a) *blow* means "(to move) in a burst of air". The *off* is actually a preposition that is tied to the noun phrase *the sidewalk*. The other meaning, in (b), is the colloquial expression *blow off* meaning "didn't do", "ignored responsibilities", or "didn't show up" in some circumstances. Phrases like *blow off* or *blow up* often allow two orders of the object and the particle (*off* or *up*): *I blew up the building* and *I blew the building up*.

Now consider the following sentences:

c) Sean blew him off.
d) Sean blew off him.

Question 1: What meaning(s) does sentence (c) have? Are they different from sentence (d)? Is sentence (d) even grammatical in your dialect?

Question 2: Now you get to use Google® or a similar search engine to investigate the frequency of phrases like (a–d) to see if their relative frequencies correspond to the availability of meanings. Perform the following steps:

1) Go to Google.com® or a similar search engine.
2) Click on "advanced search" (you may have to click on the "gear" icon at the top right).
3) In the box labeled "This exact wording or phrase" type in the following phrases, then hit "search". (Using the normal search function won't work. You need to use the "exact wording" option.)
   i) "blow the guy off"
   ii) "blow off the guy"

---

[2] It can also have a third, sexually charged, meaning. I emphatically want you to ignore that possibility here.

     iii)   "blow him off"

     iv)   "blow off him"

4) Note down the number of hits for each search. (In Google®, this number appears at the top of the search results right under the search bar.)

5) Next, calculate the percentages of (i) vs. (ii) (*Blow the guy off* vs. *blow off the guy*). To do this take each number, divide it by the total number of hits of (i) and (ii) summed together, then multiply the result by 100.

6) Next calculate the percentages of (iii) vs. (iv).

Is there is a big difference between the percentage of examples like (iv) and the percentage of examples like (ii)?

Question 3: Is there a correspondence between the numbers you got above and your judgments of grammaticality and meaning?

Question 4: Look at the first few pages of your search results for "blow off him". Do any of these have the "didn't bother to show up" meaning? What does this tell you about the structure of sentence (d)?

WBE4.   SEMANTIC VS. SYNTACTIC JUDGMENTS
[Application of Knowledge; Basic]

Each of the following sentences might be considered to be ungrammatical, unacceptable, or just odd. For each sentence, indicate whether the ungrammaticality or oddness has to do with syntax (form) or semantics (meaning) or both.

a) The chocolate-covered sausage sincerely wanted her mother-in-law to leave.

b) What do you wonder who chased?

c) Cat the dog the bark at.

d) Andrew is a professor and not a professor.

e) Danced makes me to have tired.

ANSWERS

WBE1.   PRESCRIPTIVE RULES

Part 1:

a) This sentence ends in a preposition. Prescriptively it should be *In(to) what did you put the present?*

b) The complement of a comparative is supposed to be in the nominative case. Prescriptively, this should be *She's smarter than he.* The reasoning is that the sentence is really a shortening of *She's smarter than he is.*

c) This sentence has a split infinitive (*to boldly go*). Prescriptively, this should be *To go boldly where no man has gone before.*

d) *Slow* is an adjective, not an adverb, but here it modifies a verb. The prescriptively correct form is *He walks too slowly.*

e) The adverb *hopefully* is supposed to only mean "in a hopeful manner"; the weather is unlikely to be hopeful. Prescriptively it should be *I hope that the weather will turn sunny soon.*

f) The string of words that follows *something* is a restrictive relative clause and should be introduced by *that*. An alternate non-restrictive meaning could be forced by inserting a comma before the *which*. Prescriptively this should *be I found out something that will disturb you greatly.*

g) *Who* represents the object of the verb *see*, so should be in the accusative form *whom* (*Whom did you see?*).

h) This one is hard for American speakers to spot. *Hardly* is a negative adverb, so this is seen as a case of double negation. In prescriptive terms it should be *I can hardly sleep.*

i) *Less* is supposed to be used with mass nouns (nouns like *water* or *air*) and *item* is not a mass noun, so prescriptively this should be *10 items or fewer.*

j) The prescriptively correct form is *different from*. *Than* is supposed to be a conjunction rather than a preposition, and so can't be used to connect an adjective with a pronoun. So prescriptively this should be *My view of grammar is different from yours.*

k) At least in prescriptive British English, the correct future auxiliary that is used with first person subjects (i.e., *I, we*) is *shall*, not *will*. So this should be *I shall not enjoy it.*

l) When the word *if* marks a counterfactual conditional (i.e., it is used to describe a state of being that isn't actually true), then the verb should be in its subjunctive form. So this sentence would be *If I were a linguist, then I wouldn't have to study prescriptive rules.*

m) Prescriptive grammarians tell us to avoid passives. Sentence (m) is a passive. The active form of this would be something like *You didn't complete the homework efficiently.*

n) According to prescriptive grammar *each other* is only supposed to be used when there are two participants, so "proper" grammar would have this as *All of the linguists at the conference congratulated one another.*

o) *Me* is the accusative form of the pronoun, so it's supposed to be used only in object positions or after a preposition. In this sentence, the pronoun is in the subject position so it's supposed to be the nominative *I*. The order of the noun *John* and the pronoun is also reversed from prescriptive order. The "correct" form for this sentence is *John and I are going to the movies later.*

p) The conjunction *like* is supposed to mean "similar to" rather than "as an example". So the prescriptive interpretation of this sentence is one where the speaker wants to learn a language that's similar to French, but not French itself. Prescriptively, if you intend an "as an example" meaning you're supposed to use *such as* instead of *like*: *I want to learn a new language, such as French.*

Part 2: The answer to this part of the question will be a personal one. You might truly find some of these sentences unacceptable, but others you might be surprised are judged "wrong" at all. Personally, I find my inner voice balks a bit at (d), (f), and (l). However, the rest sound like things I say every day. This said, from a descriptive point of view, you will find that native speakers of English will all utter sentences like these "ungrammatical" ones. In many cases, they're probably far more common in actual speech and writing than the "correct" forms. So if we're being scientists we're going to want to concentrate on what people actually do rather than on what so-called experts tell us to do.

WBE2. SCIENTIFIC METHOD PRACTICE

Question 1: Sentence (d) is predicted by the hypothesis: The first word in the declarative/statement form is the second word in the *Y/N* question, and vice versa.

Question 2: Sentence (f), however, is not predicted: it is the fourth word of sentence (e) that appears first in the question.

Question 3: Hypothesis 1 predicts that the *yes/no* question form of sentence (9) would be **Old the hobbit will eat the magic beans*. The second word (*old*) is inverted with the first (*the*).

Question 4: Hypothesis 2 should be something like "*Yes/No* questions are formed by moving the auxiliary of the equivalent declarative sentence to the front" or "*Yes/No* questions are formed by reversing the positions of the subject and the auxiliary." Your wording may vary.

WBE3. USING CORPORA FOR DOING SYNTACTIC RESEARCH

Question 1: For me, sentence (d) is only grammatical with a lot of context (see the sentences in answer to Question 4 below), but to the extent it's okay, it has to mean that Sean puffed air across him. Sentence (c) by contrast is completely grammatical and can mean either "Sean didn't show up for their meeting" or "Sean used a puff of air to clear all the dust off of him".

Question 2: Because of the way Google® and search engines like it work, the exact numbers for this experiment will vary from day to day. But the general pattern of effect should be found no matter when the experiment is done. Here are the results

I got on June 10, 2011. The numbers are not exact, as Google only offers an approximation once the numbers get large enough.

i)	"blow the guy off"	12100	31.1% (of i + ii)
ii)	"blow off the guy"	26800	68.9% (of i + ii)
iii)	"blow him off"	3,330,000	90.2% (of iii + iv)
iv)	"blow off him"	363,000	9.8% (of iii + iv)

You'll notice that one of these numbers is very different from the others. Although there is a clear difference between the statistical frequency of (i) and (ii), the form with the pronoun *him* following the *off* (iv) is significantly less frequent than that where it precedes *off* (iii). Furthermore, note that the percentages are in the reverse proportion to those of (i) and (ii): "off + N" order is more frequent with a full noun, but the reverse order (pronoun + off) is far more frequent when we have a pronoun instead of a noun phrase like "the guy".

Question 3: There seems to be a correspondence between our judgments of meaning and the statistics here. The form most English speakers either find ungrammatical or consider to have a very limited and non-idiomatic meaning, i.e. (iv), is also the statistically rarest in the giant corpus known as the Web.

Question 4: The first three most relevant/popular hits I got were the following:

e) As he walks up the stairs in the giant mansion, his thin linen clothes blow off him in a stiff breeze.[3]

f) The skunk sprayed Bill with its strongest scent. Bill's mother had to hang Bill on the clothesline for a week to let the smell blow off him.[4]

g) Watching Warren's skin blow off him like an unzipped windbreaker in a brutal, gale-force breeze was just… ewww.[5]

Clearly all of these examples intend the meaning where there is air blowing around. This suggests clearly that *blow off him* is always interpreted where the "off" is a preposition that takes an object noun (i.e., [blow [off him]]). The fourth most important hit I got, (h), does have the "ignore" idiomatic meaning, but the *him* is actually the subject of an embedded gerundive clause, suggesting that this is a different animal from (e–g) above.

h) I would just blow off [him saying he likes you for now].[6]

The rest of the hits on the first page have the "puff of air" meaning seen in sentences (e–f), and a quick skim of the rest of the pages of hits shows that sentence (h) is an anomaly.

---

[3] http://blogs.philadelphiaweekly.com/music/2011/06/01/countdown-to-r-kelly-the-man-plays-the-mann-in-33-days/.

[4] http://www.pittsfordschools.org/webpages/rzogby/files/pecos%20bill.pdf.

[5] http://www.ew.com/ew/article/0,,237965,00.html.

[6] http://uk.answers.yahoo.com/question/index?qid=20110513125104AAThGmN.

What does this mean for us as syntacticians? Sometimes corpora can be used to verify judgments we have about structure. But the statistics don't get at one important fact about the sentences above: The rare form is restricted in meaning as well.

WBE4.   SEMANTIC VS. SYNTACTIC JUDGMENTS

a)   Semantically odd. Sausages don't have mothers-in-law (among other strange things about this sentence).
b)   This is semantically hard to understand, but it's probably due to a syntactic effect. English doesn't typically allow you to have multiply displaced questions words like *what* and *who*.
c)   Syntactic. The order of the words is clearly wrong.
d)   Semantically strange. This is a contradiction. Andrew can't both be professor and not a professor at the same time. (Although I'm not always doing syntax in real life!)
e)   There are a couple of syntactic peculiarities here. *Danced* is either a past tense or a past participle and shouldn't appear as the subject of the sentence (we might expect *dancing* instead). In English (but not in many other languages), you don't "have tired"; you "are tired". Finally, *make* typically doesn't take a non-finite clause (marked by the *to*). We expect something more like *Dancing makes me tired*. Note that the sentence is perfectly comprehensible and meaningful, even though it's not a sentence that any native speaker of English would ever utter.

part 1

Preliminaries

chapter 2

Parts of Speech

WORKBOOK EXERCISES

WBE1.   LUMMI[1]
[Data Analysis: Intermediate]

Consider the following data from Lummi (Straits Salish).[2] Assume that (a) *t'iləm-lə-sx^w* is a verb. What part of speech are the (b) and (c) forms? Don't worry about all the unusual letters and diacritics; they are irrelevant to your answer. Pay attention to the meaning of the suffixes that are attached to each word (*-lə*, which means past, and *-sx^w*, which means second person singular subject).

a)   t'iləm-lə-sx^w
     sing-PAST-2SG.NOM
     "You sang."   verb
b)   si'em-lə-sx^w
     chief-PAST-2SG.NOM
     "You were a chief."   _____

---

[1]   Several of the problem sets in this section of the workbook are loosely based on ones found in Carnie (2011) and are used with the permission of the author – that would be me, by the way.
[2]   Data from Jelinek and Demers (1994).

The Syntax Workbook, First Edition. Andrew Carnie.
© 2013 Andrew Carnie. Published 2013 by John Wiley & Sons, Inc.

c)   sey̓si-lə-sxʷ
     afraid-PAST-2SG.NOM
     "You were afraid."   _____

WBE2.   IDENTIFYING PARTS OF SPEECH
[Data Analysis; Basic]

In the following passage,[3] underline all the nouns, circle all the verbs, put a box around all the adjectives, and put a dotted underline under any adverbs.

"If you'll watch my feet, you'll see how I do it," said she; and lifting her skirt above her dainty ankles, glided across the floor on tiptoe, as lightly as a fawn at play. But Sidney Trove was not a graceful creature. The muscles on his lithe form, developed in the school of work or in feats of strength, at which he had met no equal, were untrained in all graceful trickery. He loved dancing and music and everything that increased the beauty and delight of life, but they filled him with a deep regret of his ignorance.

WBE3.   FUNCTIONAL PARTS OF SPEECH
[Data Analysis; Basic]

Go through the passage in exercise 2 above and see if you can tell what words are functional words. Are they all closed class?

WBE4.   PREPOSITIONS
[Data Analysis; Basic]

Identify the prepositions in the following sentences

a)   Dave ran to the cave.
b)   Sumayya hid her taxes from the federal government.
c)   Jeff put his paper under my coffee cup.
d)   Dan saw the tall-ships over the horizon.
e)   Art cleaned the pipe without an air compressor.
f)   Jennifer likes to sit by the seashore.
g)   Heidi bobbed above the waterline.
h)   Leila presented her paper before the princess.
i)   Jerid smoked every day after work.
j)   Sylvia trudged through the bog.
k)   Jorge was seen near the student union building.
l)   Calvin knocked the clock off the bedside table.
m)   Shannon bought a piano for his son.

---

[3]   Bacheller (1903).

n) Dainon jumped head first into the hot tub.
o) Alex gasped during the shocking concert.
p) Jenny jumped across the lobby.
q) Kimberley hasn't eaten since Friday.
r) Alina didn't wait until 5 pm.
s) Marian got sick at the hot dog stand.

WBE5. DETERMINERS
[Data Analysis; Basic]

Go back to the passage in exercise 2 above. How many articles, quantifiers, and deictic markers can you find? Be very careful: the *that* in the last sentence is *not* a deictic marker (it is a complementizer – which we return to below).

WBE6. CONJUNCTIONS AND COMPLEMENTIZERS
[Data Analysis; Basic]

In each of the following sentences there is a blank. Fill in the appropriate conjunction or complementizer. More than one form is possible for many of the sentences. Indicate whether the form you used is a conjunction (Conj) or complementizer (C).

a) Mark ___ Susan cut down the tree.
b) I wonder ____ Mark cut down the tree.
c) I'm sure ____ Mark cut down the tree.
d) ____ Mark cut down the tree ____ Susan did.
e) Bill asked _____ Mark cut down the tree.
f) _____ Mark cut down the tree _____ I'll be really angry.
g) Mark cut down the tree ____ Susan didn't.

WBE7. TENSE CATEGORIES
[Data Analysis; Basic]

Identify any modals, infinitive markers, or auxiliaries in the following sentences. In at least one sentence there is no modal/infinitive marker/auxiliary category; instead, the tense is marked directly on the verb.

a) Alicia will make the coffee.
b) Mary-Lou was plotting a new adventure.
c) Maria has found a new obsession.
d) Paul did not order his usual.
e) Muriel wants to eat very soon.
f) Frank could always trick us.

g) Paul is usually doing his syntax readings around this time of day.
h) I might need a new computer monitor.
i) Holly should answer her phone when I call.
j) Connie often uses email.

WBE8.   COUNT VS. MASS NOUNS I
[Data Analysis; Basic]

For each of the words below indicate whether it can occur with the quantifier *much* or the quantifier *many*.

a) pencils   b) ineptitude   c) air   d) cats   e) water   f) sugar

WBE9.   COUNT VS. MASS NOUNS II
[Data Analysis; Intermediate]

Determine whether the following nouns are mass nouns, plural count nouns, or singular count nouns. Some of these may fall into more than one category, but don't change the endings of the words (i.e., do not turn *cow* into *cows*).

a) cow   b) people   c) corn   d) dogs   e) cattle

WBE10.   SUBCATEGORIES OF VERBS
[Data Analysis; Intermediate]

Try to determine what subcategory the following verbs belong to. Use the categories in (32) in the main textbook.

a) sleep   b) rub   c) demand

ANSWERS

WBE1.   LUMMI

Both (b) and (c) are also verbs. We can tell this by virtue of the fact that they bear the same basic inflection as the verb. This tells us that semantic definitions aren't valid, because presumably the words that mean the same thing in English are nouns and adjectives respectively.

WBE2. IDENTIFYING PARTS OF SPEECH

Nouns: The following are pronouns, which are a kind of noun: *you('ll), my, I, she, her, his, he, him, they.* Clear nouns are *feet, skirt, ankles, floor, tiptoe, fawn, Sidney Trove, creature, muscles, form, school, work, feats, strength, equal, trickery, music, everything, beauty, delight, life, regret, ignorance. Play* and *dancing* are also nouns in this sentence even though they express actions.

    Verbs: For the moment I'll leave auxiliary verbs like *will* or *had* out of the list. We'll return to these later. The following are clear verbs: *watch, see, do, said, lifting, glided, was, developed, met, (were,) loved, increased, filled.*

    Adjectives: dainty, graceful, lithe, deep. Untrained is also an adjective, but this may not be obvious from the criteria listed in the main textbook.

    Adverbs: lightly. How is also an adverb, but this may not be obvious from the criteria listed in the main textbook.

WBE3. FUNCTIONAL PARTS OF SPEECH

if, ('ll for will), do, above, across, and, on, as, a, was, not, the, in, the, of, or, at, which, had, no, were, all, that, but, with.

    Yes, they are all closed class.

WBE4. PREPOSITIONS

a)	to	b)	from	c)	under	d)	over	e)	without	f)	by
g)	above	h)	before	i)	after	j)	through	k)	near	l)	off
m)	for	n)	into	o)	during	p)	across	q)	since	r)	until
s)	at										

WBE5. DETERMINERS

Articles: *the* 4, *a* 3; deictic articles 0; quantifiers: *all* 1, *every*(thing) 1.

WBE6. CONJUNCTIONS AND COMPLEMENTIZERS

a) *and* or *or*; Conj; b) *if* or *whether*; C; c) *that*; C; d) *either ... or* or *neither ... nor*; Conj; e) *if* or *whether*; C; f) *if ... then* or *either ... or* or *... nor*; Conj; g) *but*; Conj

WBE7.   Tense Categories

a) *will*
b) *was*
c) *has*
d) *did*
e) *to* (and tense is also indicated on *wants*).
f) *could* (note that *always* is an adverb not T; you can put it at the end of the sentence, unlike normal T elements).
g) *is* (again note that *usually* is not of category T; it's an adverb; you can put it at the end of the sentence, unlike normal T elements).
h) *might*
i) *should*
j) There is no independent T category here. Tense is indicated on the verb *uses*. *Often* is not a T element, it's an adverb. You can tell this because it can be shifted to the end of the sentence (*Connie uses email often*). You can't do that with normal T elements (**Maria found a new obsession has*). We will return to what happens to T in sentences like this in chapter 9.

WBE8.   Count vs. Mass Nouns I

Much can appear with *ineptitude*, *air*, *sugar*, and *water*; these are all mass nouns. *Many* can appear with *pencils* and *cats*; these are count nouns.

WBE9.   Count vs. Mass Nouns II

a) *Cow* is a singular count noun in its usual usage. It might be used in a mass context with enough imagination (i.e., there is a horrible highway accident and the mangled remains of several cows are scattered everywhere, and the police say, "We really have to clean all this cow off the road".
b) *People* is a plural count noun. It cannot be a mass noun (*much people).
c) *Corn* can be both a count noun (*Pass me a corn* (on the cob)) and a mass noun (*Corn is used to make corn syrup. Is there much corn in that soup?*).
d) *Dogs* is a plural count noun.
e) *Cattle* is a mass noun. In standard usage it cannot be used as a count noun, although for many Americans a count noun usage (synonymous with singular *cow* or *head of cattle*) is coming into use.

WBE10. SUBCATEGORIES OF VERBS

a) $V_{[NP\_]}$ (intransitive)
b) $V_{[NP\_NP]}$ (transitive type 1)
c) $V_{[NP\_\{NP/CP\}]}$ (transitive type 2)

chapter 3

Constituency, Trees, and Rules

WORKBOOK EXERCISES

WBE1.   TREES: NPs, AdjPs, and AdvPs
[Application of Skills; Basic]

Draw the trees for the following AdjPs, AdvPs, and NPs:

a)   the noisy disruptive children
b)   the very nosey flatfooted professor
c)   unclothed dancers
d)   far too honest
e)   the extremely rude officer
f)   the rather disgusting very old banana peel

WBE2.   TREES II: ENGLISH PPs
[Application of Skills; Basic]

Draw the trees for the following English NPs and PPs:

a)   under his desk

The Syntax Workbook, First Edition. Andrew Carnie.
© 2013 Andrew Carnie. Published 2013 by John Wiley & Sons, Inc.

b) the flag on the pole in the square near the legislature
(*Assume that* near the legislature *modifies* square.)

WBE3. TREES III: ENGLISH VPS
[Application of Skills; Basic]

Draw the trees for the following English VPs. Pay careful attention to where the PP modifiers attach in the structure.

a) shredded the carrots with the big brass belt-buckle
(*Assume the shredding happened with the buckle, not that the carrots had buckles.*)
b) often reads trashy novels in the bath
c) frequently reads eloquent novels by Tolstoy
d) read a trashy novel by Tolstoy in the bath yesterday

WBE4. TREES IV: COORDINATION
[Application of Skills and Knowledge; Basic to Intermediate]

Draw the trees for the following English coordination structures:

a) the pen and pencil
b) the big pen and the yellow pencil
c) in my mouth and into my belly
d) (He) ate pizza and guzzled beer.
(*You only need to draw the VP here, don't worry about* he.)
e) He went to Paris but she went to Rome.

WBE5. TREES V: ENGLISH SENTENCES
[Application of Skills and Knowledge; Basic to Intermediate]

Using the phrase structure rules you learned in this chapter, draw the trees and bracketed diagrams for the following sentences. You may want to consult the section in the book on drawing trees before attempting this problem set.

a) The very pink pumpkin squashed the ant with the broken leg.
b) People with money frequent exclusive stores.
(frequent *here is being used as a verb.*)
c) The crazy dog licked the ice-cream from the cone.
d) Marlita asked if Ryan bought new shoes.
e) The very bright light shone on the head of the suspect.
f) The handsome young hooligan will smash the car with a hammer.
(*Assume that the hooligan used the hammer, not that the car had a hammer.*)

WBE6.   AMBIGUITY 1: INSIDE NPs
[Application of Skills and Knowledge; Intermediate]

Consider the following NP. It is ambiguous.

the daughter of the officer with the pink hat

Part 1: What are the two meanings? Give paraphrases.
Part 2: Draw two trees that show the two meanings for this phrase.

WBE7.   EWE
[Data Analysis; Basic]

Consider the following data[1] from Ewe, a Kwa language spoken in Ghana.

1)	Uwa ye xa amu.	The chief looked at a child.
2)	Uwa ye xa ufi.	The chief looked at a tree.
3)	Uwa xa ina ye.	A chief looked at the picture.
4)	Amu xa ina.	A child looked at a picture.
5)	Amu ye vo ele ye.	The child wanted the chair.
6)	Amu xa ele ye.	A child looked at the chair.
7)	Ika vo ina ye.	A woman wanted the picture.

a)   Is there a word meaning "at" in Ewe or is "at" part of the verb (in other words, does the expression "look at" translate as one or two words in Ewe)?

b)   Is there a word meaning "a" in Ewe?

c)   Identify the meaning and part of speech of each of the Ewe words.

d)   What is the NP rule of Ewe?

e)   What is the VP rule of Ewe?

f)   What is the TP rule of Ewe?

g)   Draw the tree for sentence (5).

WBE8.   NEO-ARAMAIC[2]
[Data Analysis; Basic]

Consider the following sentences from Neo-Aramaic, which is spoken by people whose ancestors lived east of the Tigris in Iraq and Iran, and many of whom now live in Turkey,

---

[1]   Data from Fromkin and Rodman (1978).

[2]   The data for this question are taken from Doron and Khan (2011). The glosses have been slightly modified for pedagogical purposes.

Syria, and Israel. PERF stands for perfective, a special kind of aspect marker, IMPERF stands for imperfective. The perfective marking is irrelevant to the question.

1) Brati   quima.
   daughter.my   rose.PERF
   "My daughter rose."

2) Kalba   nwəxle.
   dog   bark.PERF
   "The dog barked."

3) Baruxăwali   baxtăke   garšiwala.
   friends.my   woman.the   pull.IMPERF
   "My friends were pulling the woman."

Now answer the following questions:

a) Is there any evidence for a determiner category in Neo-Aramaic? What about possessive pronouns?
b) Based solely on the limited evidence from the data given above, what is the NP rule of Neo-Aramaic?
c) What is the VP rule of Neo-Aramaic?
d) What is the TP rule of Neo-Aramaic?
e) Draw the trees for (2) and (3).

WBE9.   FRENCH

[Data Analysis; Intermediate]

Consider the following data from French, a Romance language spoken in France, Quebec, and various parts of Africa and Asia.[3]

1) Le   gouvernement grec   approuve le   plan d'   austérité.
   the   government   Greek   approves the   plan of   austerity
   "The Greek Government approves the austerity plan."

2) Il   a   passé   un   deuxième nuit   en   Montréal.
   He   has   spent   a   second   night   in   Montreal
   "He has spent a second night in Montreal."

3) Le   gouvernement syrien rejette toute ingérence   dans ses affaires
   The   government   Syrian rejects all   interference in   its affaires

   intérieures.
   interior
   "The Syrian government rejects all interference in its interior affairs."

---

³   Some of the sentences in this problem set are modified versions of the headlines and ledes in various articles
    from June 22, 2011 in the online version of the French newspaper *Le Monde* (http://lemonde.fr).

4)	Le	ministre	des	affaires	étrangères	italien	avait	réclamé	une
	the	minister	of[4]	affairs	foreign	Italian	had	declared	a

suspension	immédiate	des	hostilités	en	Libye.
suspension	immediate	of	hostilities	in	Libya

"The Italian minister of foreign affairs had declared an immediate suspension of hostilities in Libya."

Keep in mind the following things:

- If you speak French, try to limit yourself to the data above; adding additional data may make your answers deviate from the ones given at the end of this chapter.
- Assume there is a rule that says AdjP → Adj (we'll ignore the existence of adverbs for the purposes of this exercise).
- Note that the sentence in (4) is split onto two lines.
- Keep in mind that if an element belongs to a constituent in English, it probably belongs to the same constituent in French, even if the order is different.

Now answer the following questions about French phrase structure.

a) Are determiners optional in French? Which examples show you this?
b) What is the NP rule for French? You'll need to include determiners, AdjPs, PPs and the head N in this rule. Note that not all adjectives appear in the same place (compare (1) to (2)). Also be very cautious about the strings of adjectives in (4) – pay careful attention to what is modifying what.
c) What is the PP rule of French?
d) What is the VP rule of French?
e) What is the TP rule of French?
f) Draw the trees for all the sentences.

WBE10.   Latvian
[Data Analysis; Intermediate]

Consider the following data from Latvian,[5] a Baltic language spoken in Latvia. Glosses have been simplified for the purposes of this problem set. The following abbreviations are used: PL = plural, DEF = definite (the), INDEF = indefinite (a/an).

1)	Ātrs	suns	skrien.
	fast.INDEF	dog	run

"A fast dog is running."

---

4   *Des* actually means "of the", but ignore that for the purposes of this question.
5   Thanks to Uldis Balodis who graciously provided me with this data on a very quick turnaround.

2) Ātrais   suns   skrien.
   fast.DEF   dog   run
   "The fast dog is running."

3) Skaistas   pūces   medī   sīkus   meža   dzīvniekus.
   beautiful.INDEF   owl.PL   hunt   tiny.PL.INDEF forest   animal.PL
   "Beautiful owls are hunting tiny forest creatures."

4) Šīs   skaistās   pūces   medī   sīkos   meža   dzīvniekus.
   these   beautiful.DEF   owl.PL   hunt   tiny.PL.DEF forest   animal.PL
   "These beautiful owls are hunting the tiny forest creatures."

5) Puikas   pērk   sarkanus   ābolus   no   augļu   pārdevēja.
   boy.PL   buy   red.PL.INDEF apple.PL   from   fruit.PL seller
   "(The) boys are buying red apples from the fruit seller."

a) Look carefully at sentences (1) and (2). Where is definiteness indicated in the sentence? Do these sentences provide evidence for a determiner category in Latvian?

b) No matter what your answer to (a), is there other evidence for a determiner category in Latvian?

c) Assume there is an AdjP → Adj rule. What is the NP rule of Latvian?

d) What is the PP rule of Latvian?

e) What is the VP rule of Latvian?

f) What is the TP rule of Latvian? Is there any evidence for a T category in this data (i.e., are there any auxiliaries?)

g) Draw the trees for sentences (4) and (5).

WBE11. CHICHEŴA
[Data Analysis; Intermediate/Advanced]

Consider the following data taken from Mchombo (2004) from the Bantu language Chicheŵa.

1) Mikángo   ikusáká   zigawénga.
   lions   hunt.PRES   terrorists
   "The lions are hunting the terrorists."

2) Asodzi   adzábá   mikángo   yanú.
   fishermen steal.FUT   lions   your
   "The fishermen will steal your lions."

3) Anyani   akufúná   kutí   mikángo   idzáb   mikanda.
   baboons   want   that   lions   steal.FUT.SUBJUNCTIVE beads
   "The baboons want that the lions will steal some beads."

Using this limited data answer the following questions.

a)   Assume *yanú* is a determiner. What is the NP rule for Chicheŵa?
b)   What is the VP rule for Chicheŵa? (Stick to the data given.) Assume that the string of words following "want" is a CP.
c)   What are the TP and CP rules for Chicheŵa?
d)   Draw the trees for sentences (2) and (3).

ANSWERS

WBE1.   TREES: NPs, ADJPs, AND ADVPs

a)

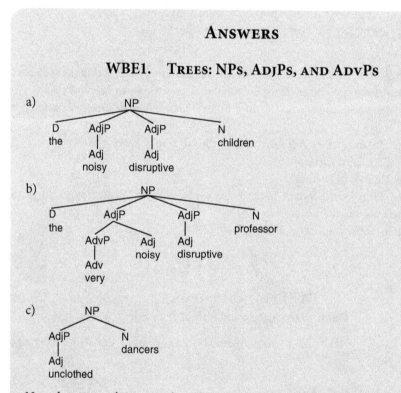

b)

c)

Note that you can't just put the Adj category right under the NP. This is because the NP rule requires an AdjP, not an Adj!

d)

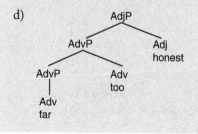

e)

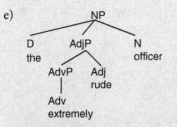

f) If you find this NP hard to accept, try putting a slight pause right after *disgusting* as if there were a comma there. There are at least three possible trees for this phrase. One possible tree for this phrase treats *banana peel* as a compound noun:

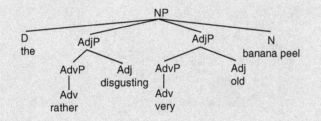

The other two trees treat *banana* as an adjective that modifies *peel*. The first version of this has *very old* modifying *peel* (i.e., an old peel of a banana).

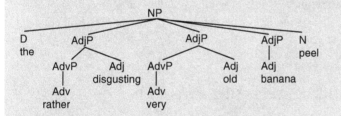

The last (probably least likely) tree, has *very old* modifying *banana* rather than *peel* (i.e. the peel of an old banana). Notice that to meet the phrase structure rules we're forced to change the category of *old* from an adjective to an adverb. This is suspicious and perhaps points towards the A category discussed in the previous chapter: Adjectives and adverbs are subcategories of the same larger A category and we collapse the AdjP and AdvP rule into the simpler rule AP → (AP) A.

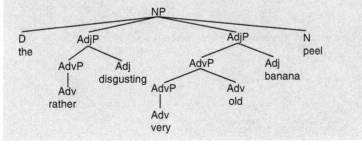

WBE2.   TREES II: ENGLISH PPs

a)

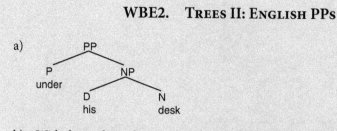

b)   With the reading where *near the legislature* modifies *square*, the tree is as follows:

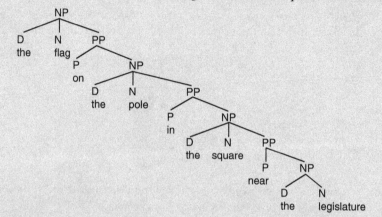

The other two possible readings (where near *the legislature* modifies either *pole* or *flag*) would have the PP *near the legislature* attached under the NPs immediately above *pole* or *flag* respectively.

WBE3.   TREES III: ENGLISH VPs

a)

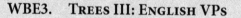
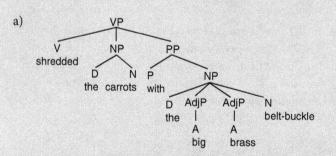

If the carrots had belt-buckles (instead of being shredded by them), then the PP would attach under the NP:

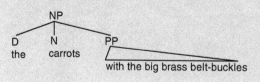

b)

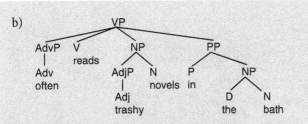

Note that the PP *trashy novels* modifies the verb *reads*, so it is attached under the VP rather than under the NP. Also note that if you have an adverb like *often*, it must be an AdvP (rather than just Adv), because the VP rule says you are allowed an AdvP in this position, not an Adv.

c)

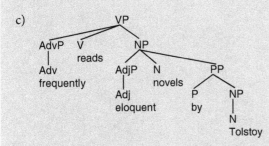

In this phrase, the PP modifies *novels*, so is attached under the NP. Compare this to the tree in (b) above.

d)

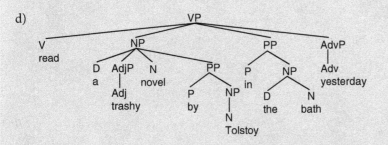

This VP has two PPs in it. One (*by Tolstoy*) modifies the N, so is attached in under the NP headed by *novel*. The other (*in the bath*) modifies the verb *read*, so is attached in under the VP.

WBE4.   TREES IV: COORDINATION

a)

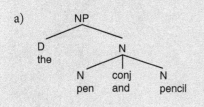

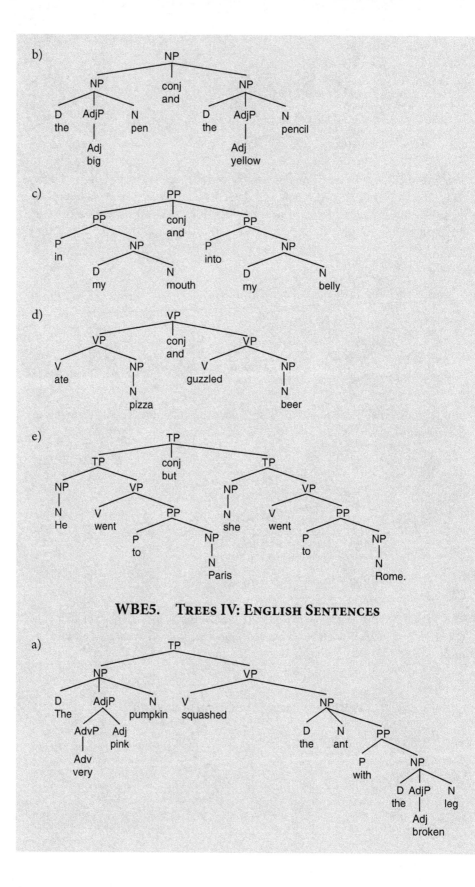

b)

```
                              NP
              ┌───────────────┼───────────────┐
             NP              conj             NP
        ┌─────┼─────┐         and        ┌─────┼─────┐
        D    AdjP    N                   D    AdjP    N
       the    │     pen                 the    │    pencil
             Adj                              Adj
             big                             yellow
```

c)

```
                              PP
              ┌───────────────┼───────────────┐
             PP              conj             PP
        ┌─────┴─────┐         and        ┌─────┴─────┐
        P          NP                    P          NP
        in      ┌──┴──┐                 into     ┌──┴──┐
                D     N                           D     N
               my    mouth                       my   belly
```

d)

```
                              VP
              ┌───────────────┼───────────────┐
             VP              conj             VP
        ┌─────┴─────┐         and        ┌─────┴─────┐
        V          NP                    V          NP
       ate          │                  guzzled      │
                    N                                N
                   pizza                            beer
```

e)

```
                                    TP
             ┌──────────────────────┼──────────────────────┐
            TP                      conj                   TP
      ┌──────┴──────┐                but          ┌─────────┴─────────┐
     NP            VP                            NP                  VP
      │       ┌─────┴─────┐                       │             ┌─────┴─────┐
      N       V          PP                       N             V          PP
      He     went    ┌────┴────┐                 she           went    ┌────┴────┐
                     P        NP                                       P        NP
                     to        │                                       to        │
                               N                                                 N
                             Paris                                             Rome.
```

WBE5.   TREES IV: ENGLISH SENTENCES

a)

```
                                    TP
                  ┌──────────────────┴──────────────────┐
                 NP                                     VP
        ┌─────────┼─────────┐                 ┌──────────┴──────────┐
        D       AdjP         N                V                    NP
       The    ┌──┴──┐      pumpkin          squashed      ┌─────────┼─────────┐
            AdvP   Adj                                    D         N         PP
             │    pink                                   the       ant    ┌────┴────┐
            Adv                                                           P        NP
            very                                                         with   ┌───┼───┐
                                                                                D AdjP  N
                                                                               the  │  leg
                                                                                   Adj
                                                                                 broken
```

[$_{TP}$ [$_{NP}$ [$_{D}$ *The*] [$_{AdjP}$ [$_{AdvP}$ [$_{Adv}$ *very*]] [$_{Adj}$ *pink*]] [$_{N}$ *pumpkin*]] [$_{VP}$ [$_{V}$ *squashed*] [$_{NP}$ [$_{D}$ *the*] [$_{N}$ *ant*] [$_{PP}$ [$_{P}$ *with*] [$_{NP}$ [$_{D}$ *the*] [$_{AdjP}$ [$_{Adj}$ *broken*]] [$_{N}$ *leg*]]]]]].

There is also a highly unlikely interpretation where the pumpkin used a broken leg as a weapon to kill the ant. This seems bizarre to me but to the extent such an interpretation is available, it would be structured by putting the PP immediately under the VP headed by *squashed* rather than under the NP headed by *ant*. However, the tree above reflects most people's intuitions about the meaning of this sentence.

b)

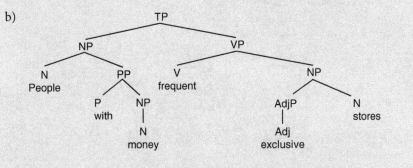

[$_{TP}$ [$_{NP}$ [$_{N}$ *People*] [$_{PP}$ [$_{P}$ *with*] [$_{NP}$ [$_{N}$ *money*]]]] [$_{VP}$ [$_{V}$ *frequent*] [$_{NP}$ [$_{AdjP}$ [$_{Adj}$ *exclusive*]] [$_{N}$ *stores*]]]]

You might find it tempting to draw the PP *with money* and the NP *exclusive stores* like the following incorrect trees:

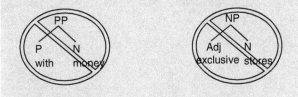

Resist these temptations! The PP rule requires an NP (PP → P **NP**); it does not allow just an N in this position, so there has to be an NP on top of the N. Similarly, the NP rule allows an AdjP, it never takes a bare Adj.

c)

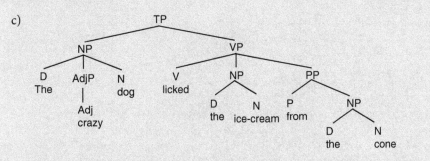

[$_{TP}$ [$_{NP}$ [$_{D}$ *The*] [$_{AdjP}$ [$_{Adj}$ *crazy*]] [$_{N}$ *dog*]] [$_{VP}$ [$_{V}$ *licked*] [$_{NP}$ [$_{D}$ *the*] [$_{N}$ *ice-cream*]] [$_{PP}$ [$_{P}$ *from*] [$_{NP}$ [$_{D}$ *the*] [$_{N}$ *cone*]]]]]

Note that unlike the tree in (a), here the PP at the end of the sentence most likely modifies the verb, so is attached under the VP rather than under the NP.

d)

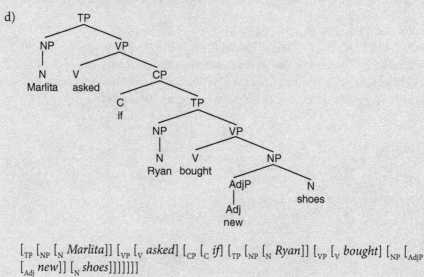

$[_{TP} [_{NP} [_{N} Marlita]] [_{VP} [_{V} asked] [_{CP} [_{C} if] [_{TP} [_{NP} [_{N} Ryan]] [_{VP} [_{V} bought] [_{NP} [_{AdjP} [_{Adj} new]] [_{N} shoes]]]]]]]]$

e)

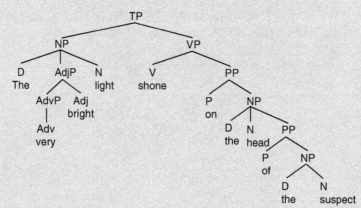

$[_{TP} [_{NP} [_{D} The] [_{AdjP} [_{AdvP} [_{Adv} very]] [_{Adj} bright]] [_{N} light]] [_{VP} [_{V} shone] [_{PP} [_{P} on] [_{NP} [_{D} the] [_{N} head] [_{PP} [_{P} of] [_{NP} [_{D} the] [_{N} suspect]]]]]]]$

f)

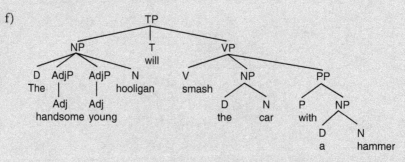

$[_{TP} [_{NP} [_{D} The] [_{AdjP} [_{Adj} handsome] [_{AdjP} [_{Adj} young]] [_{N} hooligan]] [_{T} will] [_{VP} [_{V} smash] [_{NP} [_{D} the] [_{N} car]] [_{PP} [_{P} with] [_{NP} [_{D} a] [_{N} hammer]]]]]]$

Notice that *handsome* and *young* are independently connected to the NP. This is because they both modify *hooligan*. *Handsome* does not modify *young*! (Compare to the tree in (e).)

WBE6.   AMBIGUITY 1: INSIDE NPs

Part 1:   Meaning 1: The officer is wearing a pink hat and we're talking about his daughter.
Meaning 2: The officer's daughter is wearing a pink hat.

Part 2:

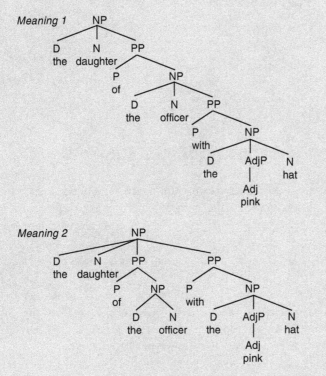

WBE7.   EWE

a)   The English two-word expression "look at" is expressed by a single word in Ewe (*xa*).
b)   No.
c)

uwa	'chief'	N
ye	'the'	D
xa	'looked at'	V
ufi	'tree'	N
ina	'picture'	N

amu	'child'	N
vo	'wanted'	V
ele	'chair'	N
ika	'woman'	N

d) NP → N (D). The determiner is optional because we find NPs without it. Other things might go in Ewe NPs, but we don't have evidence for it. Notice that the N and the D are in the reverse order from English.

e) VP → V (NP). Again, other things may well go into the VP in Ewe, but we have insufficient evidence about what they are or where they go.

f) TP → NP VP. We might presume there is an optional T, but the data given is insufficient for figuring out where that might go.

g)

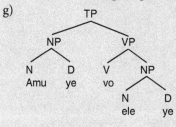

WBE8.   NEO-ARAMAIC

a) Even though there are possessive pronouns ("my") and definite determiners in the English glosses and translations, these items appear to be morphologically part of the noun in Neo-Aramaic. Therefore we won't posit a determiner category here.

b) All the NPs in this data consist of just a noun, so we can posit NP → N and nothing more.

c) The object NP in Neo-Aramaic appears before the verb (*baxtăke* comes before *garšiwala*), so that tells us the rule must be VP → (NP) V. We know the object NP is optional because it doesn't appear in sentences (1) and (2). There is not enough data here to say anything about the position of PPs or AdvPs.

d) TP → NP VP

e) 2)

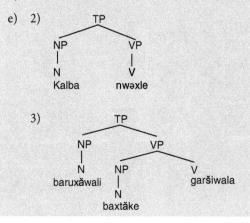

WBE9. FRENCH

a) Determiners are optional in French. We know this because of NPs like *austérité* in (1), *il* and *Montréal* in (2) and *Libye* in (4).
b) NP → (D) (AdjP) N (AdjP) (PP) (AdjP).

You need three AdjPs here because some adjectives (like *deuxième*) appear before the N, and others (like *grec* or *intérieures*) follow the noun they modify. The PP can follow the AdjP (as seen in the phrase *une suspension immediate des hostilités*), but can also appear before the AdjP, as in [*PP des affaires étrangères*] [*AdjP italien*]. Critically note that there is no evidence for a + sign after the AdjP: the two adjectives *étrangères italien* modify different nouns (*étrangères* modifies *affaires* and *italien* modifies *ministre*) so they are part of different constituents. All things being equal, we might expect that in fact a + sign is necessary (and in fact it is), but there is no data here to demonstrate that.

c) PP → P NP
d) VP → V NP (PP+)

Assuming that French has intransitive verbs (which it does) one might predict that the NP in this rule is optional. The reason we've left of the optionality parentheses here is because there is no data below that proves this. It's worth noting that the VP rule of French is likely to be as complex as the English VP rule – for example, including AdvPs – we just don't have the data here to demonstrate that, so I've left off all those complications

e) TP → NP (T) VP
f) 1)

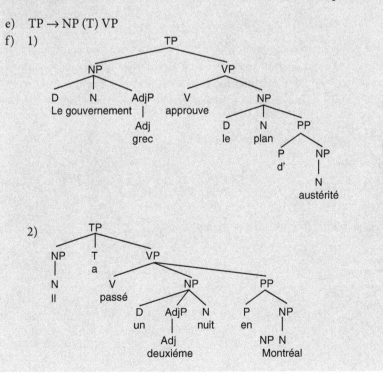

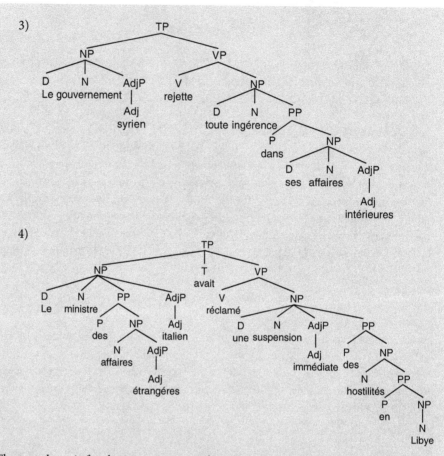

3)

4)

The tree above is for the interpretation where the hostilities in Libya are suspended. There are at least two other possible trees here. The second possible tree is the same as the first except the PP *en Libye* modifies the verb *réclamé* (i.e., where the declaration happened in Libya). In such a situation the PP would be attached as a sister to the V:

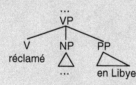

The third tree has *en Libye* modifying *suspension*:

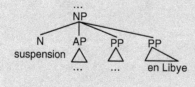

WBE10. LATVIAN

a) Definiteness in Latvian seems to be most regularly marked on adjectives, but we wouldn't want to claim that these are determiners, because in sentence (4) we have both the deictic determiner and a definitely marked adjective.

b) Yes, we have the deictic marker *šīs* in sentence (4).

c) NP → (D) (AdjP+) N. The optionality of the AdjP is shown in the subject of sentence (5). The fact that you can have multiple AdjPs is seen in the object of sentences (4) and (5).

d) PP → P NP. There is no evidence in the data about whether the NP is optional or not.

e) VP → V (NP) (PP). There is no evidence in the data about whether or not a +mark is needed after the PP.

f) TP → NP VP. There is no evidence in this data about the position of auxiliaries or a T category.

g) 4)

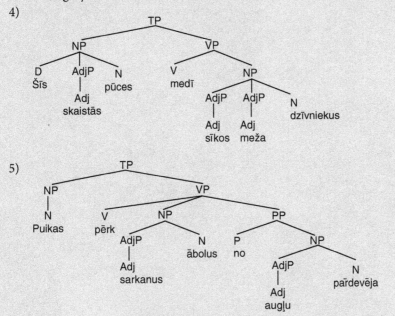

WBE11. CHICHEŴA

a) NP → N (D)

b) VP → V {NP/CP} (I haven't marked the NP/CP here as optional, but given what goes on in other languages, we might presume that they are optional just like in English.)

c) TP → NP VP (There are no examples of auxiliaries in this data, so I have not included an optional T.)

d) 1)

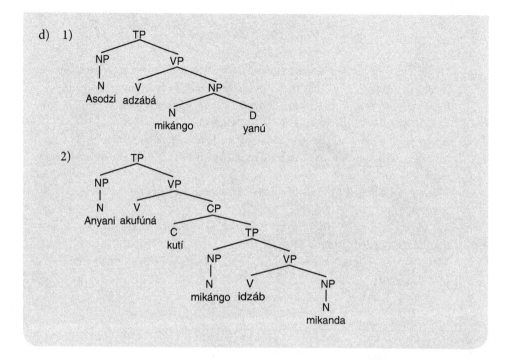

chapter 4

Structural Relations

WORKBOOK EXERCISES

EXERCISES 1 TO 9 ARE ALL BASED ON THE FOLLOWING TREE:

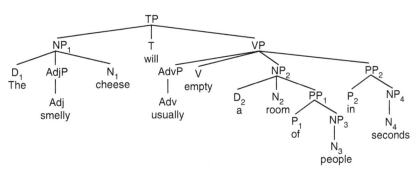

WBE1. PARTS OF A TREE
[Application of Skills; Basic]

Referring to the tree above, answer the following questions.

a)   What is the root node?

The Syntax Workbook, First Edition. Andrew Carnie.
© 2013 Andrew Carnie. Published 2013 by John Wiley & Sons, Inc.

b) What are the terminal nodes? List them all.

c) Is VP a non-terminal node?

WBE2. DOMINATION
[Application of Skills; Basic]

a) List all the nodes that NP_2 dominates.

b) What nodes dominate N_3?

c) What node dominates both N_1 and T?

d) Does V dominate any nodes?

e) What node dominates both D_2 and NP_2, but not NP_1?

WBE3. EXHAUSTIVE DOMINATION
[Application of Skills; Intermediate]

a) What node exhaustively dominates D_2, N_2, P_1, and N_3?

b) What node exhaustively dominates AdvP, V, NP_2, PP_2? (Be careful about this one. It's tricky!)

c) List the nodes that PP2 exhaustively dominates.

d) Do D_1, Adj, and N_1 form a constituent? How do you know?

e) Are V and D_2 exhaustively dominated by a node? If so, which one?

f) Is AdvP a constituent of VP?

g) Is Adj a constituent of VP?

h) Are T and V constituents of TP?

WBE4. IMMEDIATE DOMINATION
[Application of Skills; Basic]

a) What node immediately dominates D_2?

b) List all the nodes that NP_1 immediately dominates.

c) Does PP_2 immediately dominate N_4? Why or why not?

d) What node immediately dominates P_1?

e) Is PP_1 an immediate constituent of VP?

f) Is NP_4 an immediate constituent of PP_2?

g) What is the mother of D_1?

h) What are N_2's sisters?

i) Is N_3 a daughter of PP_1?

WBE5. SISTER PRECEDENCE AND PRECEDENCE
[Application of Skills; Basic]

a) Does D_1 sister-precede AdjP?

b) Does D_1 sister-precede N_1?

c) Does N_1 sister-precede T?

d) Does Adj sister-precede N_1?

e) Does AdvP sister-precede V?

f) Does NP_1 precede N_1?

g) Does VP precede NP_4?

h) Does N_1 precede AdvP? What is the pair of nodes that are in a sister-precedence relation that prove this?

i) Does NP_2 precede P_2?

WBE6.   IMMEDIATE PRECEDENCE
[Application of Skills; Intermediate]

a) Does T sister-precede AdvP?

b) Does T immediately precede AdvP?

c) Does V immediately precede D_2?

d) Does V immediately precede NP_2?

e) Does V immediately precede N_2?

f) What node immediately precedes N_3? Are these two nodes in a sister-precedence relationship?

g) What node does N_3 immediately precede?

WBE7.   C-COMMAND
[Application of Skills; Intermediate]

a) List the nodes that D_1 c-commands.

b) What node does P_1 symmetrically c-command?

c) What node does P_1 asymmetrically c-command?

d) Does NP_2 c-command D_2? Why or why not?

e) Does NP_1 c-command NP_3?

f) Does NP_3 c-command NP_1?

g) Does PP_2 c-command PP_1?

h) Does NP_4 c-command NP_3?

WBE8.   GOVERNMENT
[Application of Skills; Intermediate/Advanced]

a) Does D_1 c-command N_1?

b) D_1 does not phrase-govern N_1. Explain why not.

c) Does NP_1 phrase-govern PP_1?

d) Does T head-govern V?

e) Does T head-govern D_2?

WBE9.   GRAMMATICAL RELATIONS
[Application of Skills; Basic]

a)   What is the subject in the tree above?
b)   What is the direct object in the tree above?
c)   Is PP_2 an indirect object or an oblique? How can you tell?
d)   There are two NPs which are objects of prepositions. What are they?

WBE10.   DRAW A TREE WITH THE FOLLOWING PROPERTIES
[Application of Skills; Advanced]

Draw a tree with the following properties:

* A is a root node.
* B, C, D, E, F, and G are all terminal nodes.
* A, H, I, J, and K are non-terminal nodes.
* H dominates B, C, and D.
* B sister precedes I.
* B head-governs C.
* I immediately dominates C and D.
* C immediately precedes D.
* H immediately precedes J.
* F and G are exhaustively dominated by J.
* F symmetrically c-commands G.
* E asymmetrically c-commands F and G.
* D immediately precedes F.
* F precedes E.
* G precedes E.
* E and J are immediate constituents of K.

ANSWERS

WBE1.   PARTS OF A TREE

a)   TP
b) D_1, Adj, N_1, T, Adv, V, D_2, N_2, P_1, N_3, P_2, N_4
c)   Yes

WBE2.   DOMINATION

a) D_2, N_2, PP_1, P_1, NP_3, N_3
b) NP_3, PP_1, NP_2, VP, TP

c)   TP
d)   No
e)   VP

WBE3.   EXHAUSTIVE DOMINATION

a) NP_2
b)   None. You might have thought it was VP, but exhaustive domination holds only over terminals, so it's incoherent to talk about exhaustive domination of AdvP and NP.
c) P_2, N_4 (not NP_4, because it's not a terminal).
d)   Yes. They are exhaustively dominated by NP_1.
e)   No, there is no node that exhaustively dominates V and D_2 to the exclusion of other terminals.
f)   Yes
g)   No
h)   Yes

WBE4.   IMMEDIATE DOMINATION

a) NP_2
b)   D1, AdjP, N_1
c)   No, NP_4 gets in the way (PP_2 immediately dominates NP_4 and NP_4 immediately dominates N_4).
d) PP_1
e)   No, it's an immediate constituent of NP_2.
f)   Yes
g) NP_1
h) D_2, PP1
i)   No, it's a daughter of NP_3. (Mother–daughter relations are based on immediate dominance, not simple dominance.)

WBE5.   SISTER PRECEDENCE AND PRECEDENCE

a)   Yes
b)   Yes
c)   No
d)   No
e)   Yes
f)   No, they are in a domination relationship. If two nodes are in a domination relationship, then they can't be in a precedence relation.

g) No, it dominates it instead.

h) Yes, because NP_1 (which dominates N_1) sister-precedes VP (which dominates AdvP).

i) Yes

WBE6.   IMMEDIATE PRECEDENCE

a) No

b) Yes

c) Yes

d) Yes

e) No

f) P_1; no, they are not in a sister-precedence relationship.

g) P_2

WBE7.   C-COMMAND

a) AdjP, Adj, N_1

b) NP_3

c) N_3

d) No, because NP_2 dominates D_2, and domination excludes c-command.

e) Yes

f) No

g) Yes. Note that c-command doesn't care about precedence relations, so things on the right can c-command things on the left.

h) No, NP_4's sister is P_2 and NP_3 is not a daughter of P_2.

WBE8.   GOVERNMENT

a) Yes

b) No; they are heads not phrases.

c) No; AdvP and PP_2 both count as interveners.

d) Yes

e) No, because V intervenes.

WBE9.   GRAMMATICAL RELATIONS

a) NP_1

b) NP_2

c) It's an oblique. You can tell because *empty* is not a ditransitive verb.

d) NP_3 is the object of P_1 and NP_4 is the object of P_2.

WBE10. DRAW A TREE WITH THE FOLLOWING PROPERTIES

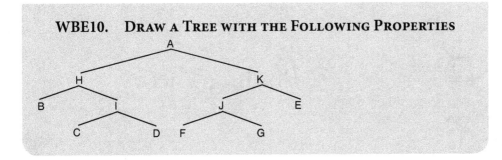

chapter 5

Binding Theory

WORKBOOK EXERCISES

WBE1.   NP TYPES
[Data Analysis; Basic]

Identify all the NPs in the following sentences and determine if they are anaphors, pronouns, or R-expressions.

a)   Maisy wandered lazily into the store so that she could buy herself some shampoo.
b)   Pangur thought that he could easily catch it.
c)   He loved giving her a hard time.
d)   I don't trust myself with a staple gun.

WBE2.   INDEXATION
[Data Analysis; Basic]

Put indexes on each of the sentences in WBE1, to show the reference of each noun. When two NPs refer to the same thing be sure to mark them with the same index. Because pronouns are sometimes ambiguous, sentences (a) and (b) actually each have two different possible indexations.

The Syntax Workbook, First Edition. Andrew Carnie.
© 2013 Andrew Carnie. Published 2013 by John Wiley & Sons, Inc.

WBE3. C-COMMAND AND BINDING
[Data Analysis; Intermediate]

a) Draw the tree for sentence (d) in WBE 1 (*I don't trust myself with a staple gun*). Assume *don't* is a T node. Annotate the tree with indices. (Note that the index goes on the NP, not the N head!)
b) Does the antecedent bind the anaphor?
c) Does the anaphor bind the antecedent?
d) Are there any other binding relationships in the tree?
e) Does this sentence meet Condition A of the binding theory?

WBE4. C-COMMAND AND BINDING II
[Data Analysis; Advanced]

Explain why the following sentence is ungrammatical:

*That Alex$_i$ always passes out after drinking orange juice irks himself$_i$.

Assume that *[That Alex always passes out after drinking orange juice]* is a CP in subject position of the clause with the VP *irks himself.*

WBE5. BINDING DOMAIN
[Data Analysis; Basic]

Each of the sentences below contains an anaphor. For each sentence, identify the anaphor, its antecedent, and the binding domain for the anaphor.

a) Calvin really loves himself.
b) Bill knows that Ken secretly hates himself.
c) The fact that Trevor is eating himself out of house and home bothers Frankie.

WBE6. PRONOUNS
[Data Analysis; Basic]

Identify the pronoun in each of the following sentences, then determine if it is bound and if so by what. Explain what the binding domain for the pronoun is, and state whether or not the pronoun is free or bound within that domain. Assume the indexing given.

a) He$_i$ left New York$_j$.
b) Peter$_i$ told him$_k$ that Bill already ate.
c) *Peter$_i$ told him$_i$ that Bill already ate.

d)   That the guy$_i$ was going home made him$_i$ happy.
e)   Bill$_i$ said that he$_i$ hated guard dogs.
f)   Bill$_i$ said that he$_k$ hated guard dogs.

WBE7.   R-EXPRESSIONS
[Data Analysis; Basic]

Identify each of the R-expressions in the following sentences. Determine if they are bound and if so by what. Assume the indexing given. Many of the sentences contain more than one R-expression.

a)   Neil wanted a new book.
b)   Sally bit Kim on the neck.
c)   Sally$_i$ bit herself$_i$ on the neck.
d)   *He$_i$ loves Bill$_i$.

ANSWERS

WBE1.   NP TYPES

a)   *Maisy*, R-expression
     the store, R-expression
     she, pronoun
     herself, anaphor
     some shampoo, R-expression
b)   *Pangur*, R-expression
     he, pronoun
     it, pronoun
c)   *He*, pronoun
     her, pronoun
     a hard time, R-expression
d)   *I*, pronoun
     myself, anaphor
     a staple gun, R-expression. (*Staple* here is either an adjective or part of a compound noun *staple-gun*.)

WBE2.   INDEXATION

a)   [Maisy]$_i$ wandered lazily into [the store]$_k$ so that [she]$_i$ could buy [herself]$_i$ [some shampoo]$_m$.

OR

[Maisy]$_i$ wandered lazily into [the store]$_k$ so that [she]$_n$ could buy [herself]$_n$ [some shampoo]$_m$.

b) [Pangur]$_i$ thought that [he]$_i$ could easily catch [it]$_m$.   OR

[Pangur]$_i$ thought that [he]$_k$ could easily catch [it]$_m$.

c) [He]$_i$ loved giving [her]$_k$ [a hard time]$_m$.

d) [I]$_i$ don't trust [myself]$_i$ with [a staple gun]$_k$.

WBE3. C-COMMAND AND BINDING

a)

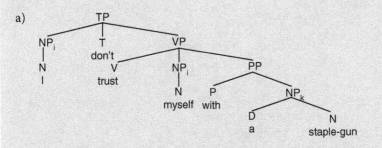

b) Yes, the two NPs are coindexed and the NP containing *I* c-commands the anaphor NP containing *himself*. Therefore, the antecedent binds the anaphor.

c) No; although they share an index, the anaphor does not c-command the NP containing *I*, so it does not bind it.

[Important note: I often hear students talking about NPs binding each other. Don't do that! Antecedents and the things they bind are always in asymmetric relations, such that the antecedent binds the anaphor or pronoun, but critically not vice versa.]

d) No, nothing else is coindexed, so there won't be any other binding no matter what the c-command relations are.

e) Yes, it meets Condition A, since the anaphor *himself* is bound by the antecedent *I*.

WBE4. C-COMMAND AND BINDING II

This is a Condition A violation, because the anaphor cannot find a c-commanding co-indexed NP antecedent. *Alex* does not c-command *himself*. If you've read ahead, you might have claimed that this was a problem with the binding domain. This is incorrect. The binding domain for the anaphor *himself* is the entire sentence, which contains the antecedent *Alex*. So the two are in the same binding domain. The problem with this sentence is c-command, not binding domain.

WBE5.   BINDING DOMAIN

a)   *Calvin* = antecedent
    himself = anaphor
    The whole sentence (TP) is the binding domain.
b)   *Ken* = antecedent
    himself = anaphor
    Binding domain = *Ken secretly hates himself* (the embedded CP).
c)   *Alicia* = antecedent
    herself = anaphor
    Binding domain = *that Alicia is eating herself out of house and home.*

WBE6.   PRONOUNS

a)   *He*$_i$ is free.
    The binding domain is the whole sentence.
b)   *Him* is free (it isn't coindexed with anything).
    The binding domain is the whole sentence.
c)   *Him* is bound by *Peter*.
    The binding domain is the whole sentence, so it is bound within its binding domain and is a violation of Condition B.
d)   While *him* is coindexed with *the guy*, it is not c-commanded by *the guy*, so it is not bound (and thus free).
    The binding domain is the whole sentence.
e)   *He* is bound by *Bill* (coindexed and c-commanded by Bill).
    The binding domain is the embedded clause, so it is free within its domain, even though it's bound.
f)   *He* is free.
    The binding domain is the embedded clause.

WBE7.   R-EXPRESSIONS

a)   *Neil* is free.
    a new book is free
b)   *Sally* is free.
    Kim is free.
    the neck is free.
c)   *Sally* is free even though it is coindexed with *herself* because it is not c-commanded by *herself.*
    the neck is free.
d)   *Bill* is bound; it is both coindexed with and c-commanded by *he*. This is a Condition C violation.

chapter 6

X-bar Theory

WORKBOOK EXERCISES

WBE1.   SPANISH NOMINAL ELLIPSIS
[Data Analysis; Basic]

Spanish has a phenomenon similar in function to English *one*-replacement. However, instead of using the word *one*, Spanish speakers simply delete part of the NP. This kind of deletion is called ***nominal ellipsis***. In sentence (1), you'll see that Spanish speakers simply omit some of the noun phrase. [Data from Kester and Sleeman 2002.]

1) Compré   la   falda negra   y   la ____ amarilla.
    bought.1s   the   skirt black   and   the ____ yellow
    "I bought the black skirt and the yellow one."

In addition to the fact that we see deletion or omission in Spanish, there is one other way that Spanish nominal ellipsis is different from English *one*-replacement. This difference is seen in example (2):

2) el libro   de Joaquín   y   el ___ de Christina
    the book   of Joaquin   and   the ____ of Christina
    "Joaquin's book and Christina's"

(or more literally "the book of Joaquin and the one of Christina")

The Syntax Workbook, First Edition. Andrew Carnie.
© 2013 Andrew Carnie. Published 2013 by John Wiley & Sons, Inc.

Concentrating on example (2), what is the difference between *one*-replacement in English and nominal ellipsis in Spanish?

WBE2. STRUCTURAL POSITIONS OF ADJUNCTS, COMPLEMENTS, AND SPECIFIERS
[Theoretical Grounding; Basic]

Keeping in mind the definitions of adjunct, complement, and specifier (e.g., the adjunct is daughter of a bar level, sister to a bar level) determine the following:

a) List all the specifiers in this abstract tree and state which head they are a specifier to.
b) List all the adjuncts in this abstract tree and state which head they are an adjunct to.
c) List all the complements in this abstract tree and state which head they are a complement to.

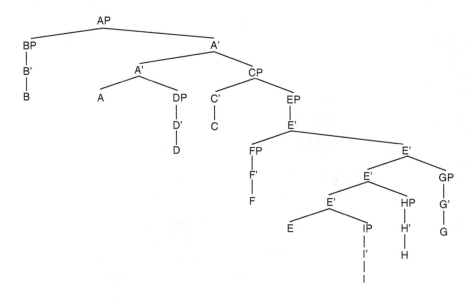

WBE3. MODIFIER TYPES: NPs
[Data Analysis; Basic]

In each of the NPs below the head is in bold italic. Identify all the things that modify that head and indicate if they are complements to the head, adjuncts to the head, or specifiers to the head. (Assume determiners are specifiers.)

a) a *car* with bad air-conditioning
b) a plastic *statue* of the Queen on his dashboard
c) the big blue *jar* of olives on the windowsill
d) the former *director* of intelligence in the US Navy
e) some *equipment* with faulty wires in the lab

WBE4.   MODIFIER TYPES: VPs
[Data Analysis; Basic]

In each of the VPs below the head is in bold italic. Identify all the things that modify that head and indicate if they are complements to the head or adjuncts to the head.

a)   ***loves*** chocolate-covered sausages
b)   ***threw*** meatballs at the wall with a spoon on Tuesday
c)   often ***eats*** spinach ice-cream in front of me
d)   ***drinks*** in the morning every day
e)   seldom eagerly ***performs*** his exercises after supper

WBE5.   MODIFIER TYPES: ADJPS, ADVPS, AND PPS
[Data Analysis; Intermediate]

In each of the AdjPs, AdvPs, and PPs below the head is in bold italic. Identify all the things that modify that head and indicate if they are complements to the head or adjuncts to the head.

a)   very ***fearful*** of the repercussions
b)   seldom ***anxious*** about the appointment (*this one might be tricky!*)
c)   very ***quietly***
d)   straight ***to*** bed
e)   right ***at*** the top

WBE6.   TREE DRAWING 1: NPS
[Data Analysis; Basic]

Draw trees for the phrases in WBE3 above using X-bar theory.

WBE7.   TREE DRAWING 2: VPS
[Data Analysis; Basic]

Draw trees for the phrases in WBE4 above using X-bar theory. In (a) treat *chocolate-covered* as a compound (i.e. a single word).

WBE8.   TREE DRAWING 3: ADJPS, ADVPS, AND PPS
[Application of Skills; Basic]

Draw trees for the phrases in WBE5 above using X-bar theory.

WBE9. TREE DRAWING 2
[Data Analysis and Application of Skills; Basic/Advanced]

Draw trees for the phrases and sentences below using X-bar theory.

a) pink bricks of hay
b) the table with the ugly lamp beside the sofa
c) Bill felt very very anxious about his test results.
d) He was reading the textbook with no glasses.
e) Each apple in the basket came with a squirmy worm.
f) The very foolish professor of linguistics from France bought a bagful of moldy clothes in bright colors from that deceitful street vendor.

WBE10. COMMON MISTAKES IN TREE DRAWING
[Application of Skills]

It's easy to make mistakes in tree drawing when you're using X-bar theory. You have to pay special attention to those "sister to" and "daughter of" definitions, and you can't forget about the principle of modification. Below are some phrases and some trees with mistakes in them. Explain what the mistakes are, then draw the correct tree.

a) people with children

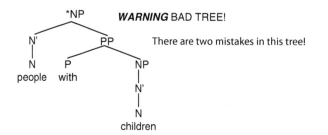

b) biked without a helmet

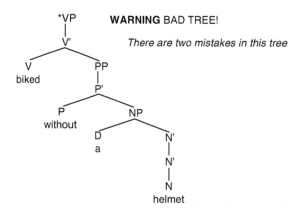

c)   bought a bike from the store on Tuesday

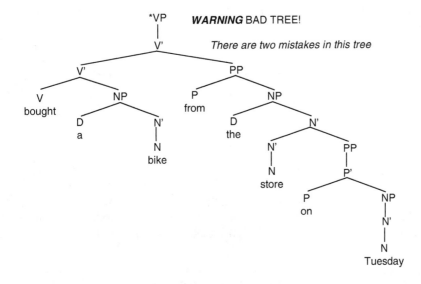

WBE11.   JAPANESE PARAMETERS[1]
[Data Analysis; Basic]

Consider the following data from Japanese:

a)   Masa-ga kita.   "Masa came."
b)   Toru-ga shinda.   "Toru died."
c)   Kumiko-ga yonda.   "Kumiko read."
d)   Kumiko-ga hon-o yonda.   "Kumiko read the book."
e)   Toru-ga Kumiko-o mita.   "Toru saw Kumiko."
f)   Kumiko-ga Toru-o mita.   "Kumiko saw Toru."
g)   Hon-ga akai desu.   "The book is red."
h)   Toru-ga sensei desu.   "Toru is a teacher."
i)   Masa-ga ookii desu.   "Masa is big."
j)   Sono hon-ga ookii desu.   "That book is big."
k)   Toru-ga sono akai hon-o mita.   "Toru saw that red book."

1)   What are the functions of the suffixes *-o* and *-ga*?
2)   What is the word order of Japanese?
3)   Does the complement precede or follow the head in Japanese?
4)   Do adjuncts precede or follow the head in Japanese?

---

[1]   Loosely based on a problem set in Akmajian and Heny (1975).

5) Do specifiers precede or follow the X' node in Japanese? Assume that *-ga* and *-o* are NOT determiners.

6) Draw the tree for sentence (k) using X-bar theory. Keep in mind your answers to questions 1–5.

ANSWERS

WBE1.   SPANISH NOMINAL ELLIPSIS

In most varieties of English, *one*-replacement can't apply before complements (**the one of chemistry*), although for some English speakers this is acceptable. Spanish seems to allow nominal ellipsis before complements such as *de Christina*. This means that nominal ellipsis in Spanish can target either N' or N nodes. The same is presumably true for those dialects of English that allow *the one of chemistry*.

WBE2.   STRUCTURAL POSITIONS OF ADJUNCTS, COMPLEMENTS, AND SPECIFIERS

a)   BP is a specifier to A.
     EP is a specifier to C. (This one is tricky because it's on the right, but it is still sister to X' and daughter of XP.)
b)   CP is an adjunct to A.
     FP is an adjunct to E.
     GP is an adjunct to E.
     HP is an adjunct to E.
c)   DP is a complement to A.
     IP is a complement to E.

WBE3.   MODIFIER TYPES: NPs

a)   *a* = specifier
     with bad air-conditioning = adjunct
b)   *a* = specifier
     plastic = adjunct
     of the queen = complement
     on his dashboard = adjunct
c)   *the* = specifier
     big = adjunct
     blue = adjunct

of olives = complement
on the windowsill = adjunct

d) *the* = specifier
former = adjunct
of intelligence = complement
in the US Navy = adjunct

e) *some* = specifier
with faulty wires = adjunct
in the lab = adjunct

WBE4. MODIFIER TYPES: VPS

a) *chocolate-covered sausages* = complement
b) *meatballs* = complement
at the wall = adjunct
with a spoon = adjunct
on Tuesday = adjunct
c) *often* = adjunct
spinach ice-cream = complement
in front of me = adjunct
d) *in the morning* = adjunct
every day = adjunct (Note that adjuncts don't have to be AdvPs or PPs!)
e) *seldom* = adjunct
eagerly = adjunct
his exercises = complement
after supper = adjunct

WBE5. MODIFIER TYPES: AdjPs, AdvPs, AND PPs

a) *very* = adjunct
of the repercussions = complement
b) *seldom* = adjunct
about the appointment = complement. Even though this PP starts with *about* rather than *of*, it "feels" like a complement. This is incredibly hard to prove however! So if you said adjunct, that's also a reasonable answer.
c) *very* = adjunct
d) *straight* = adjunct
bed = complement
e) *right* = adjunct
the top = complement

WBE6.　Tree Drawing 1: NPs

a)

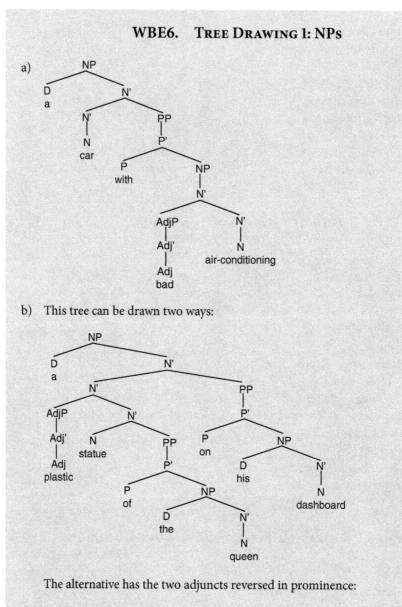

b)　This tree can be drawn two ways:

The alternative has the two adjuncts reversed in prominence:

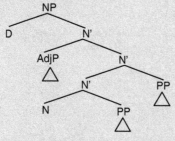

c) There are three legitimate ways to draw this tree:

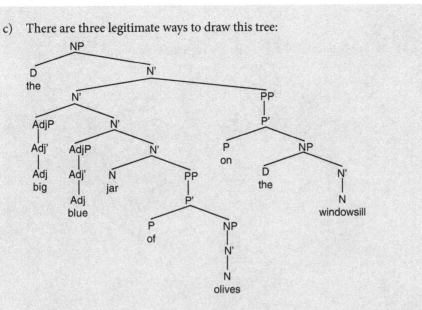

Just like the tree in (b), the adjunct PP (*on the windowsill*) can be attached in at different heights:

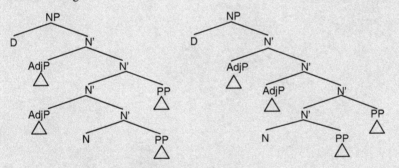

In each case, the PP is still a daughter of N' and a sister to N'.

d) This tree can be drawn two ways:

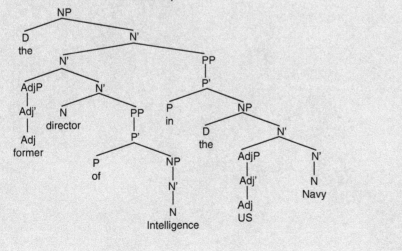

The alternative has the two adjuncts reversed in prominence:

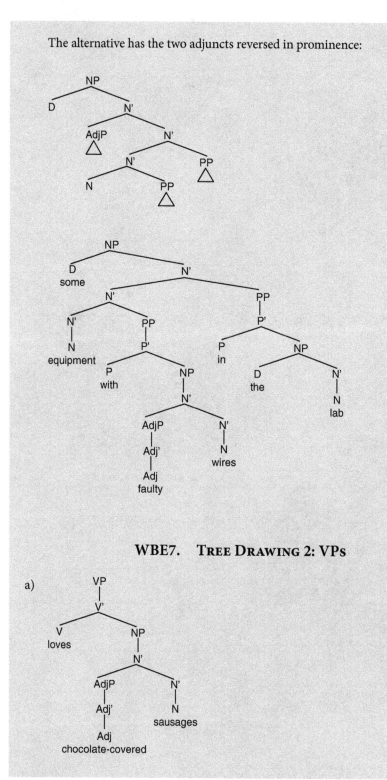

WBE7.   TREE DRAWING 2: VPs

b)

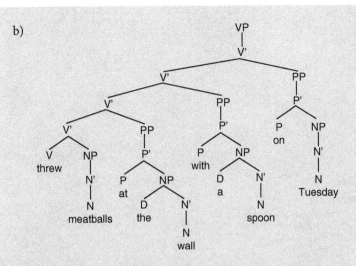

c)   There are two possible trees for this VP:

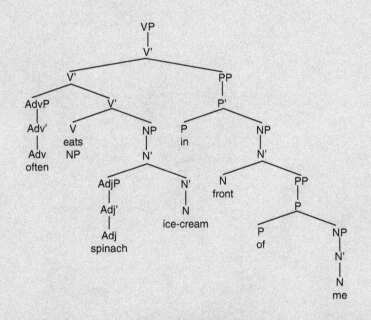

There may be an argument to be made that *spinach* is a complement to *ice-cream* or that *spinach ice-cream* is a large compound. I leave these possibilities aside in these trees. The other tree for this has the AdvP and PP adjuncts at reversed heights, both are still sister to V' and daughter of V' in this alternant.

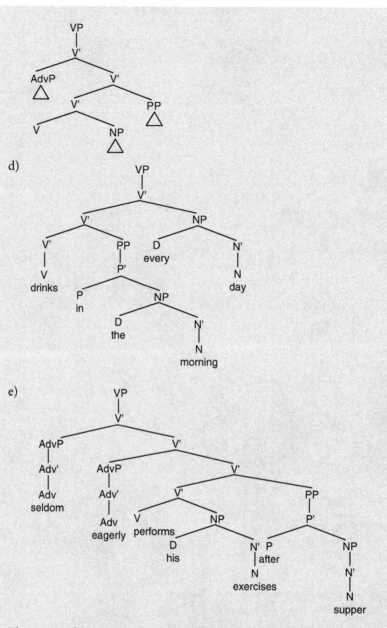

d)

e)

This tree could also be drawn with the PP attaching at any of the other V' sites:

or

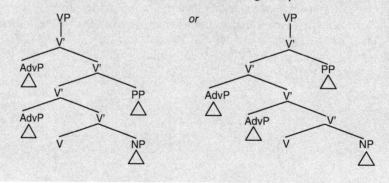

WBE8.   TREE DRAWING 3: ADJPS, ADVPS, AND PPS

a)

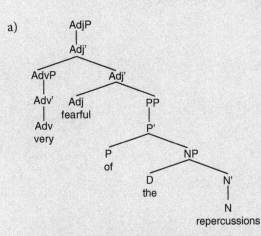

b)   I'm assuming that *about the appointment* is a complement, but that's hard to prove. It might be an adjunct, in which case there would be an additional Adj' above *anxious*:

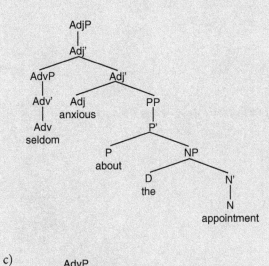

c)

d)

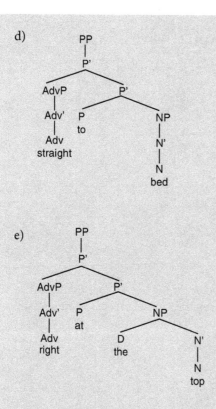

e)

WBE9.   TREE DRAWING 4: X-BAR PRACTICE

a)

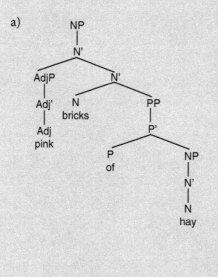

b)

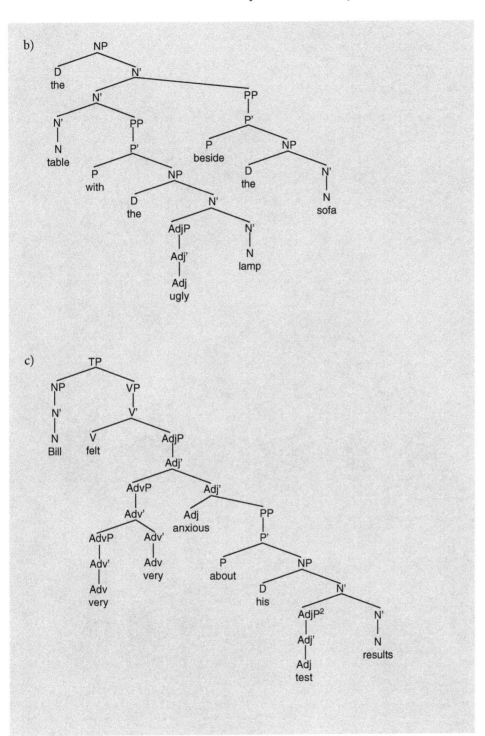

c)

2 You could also treat *test* as a noun.

d)

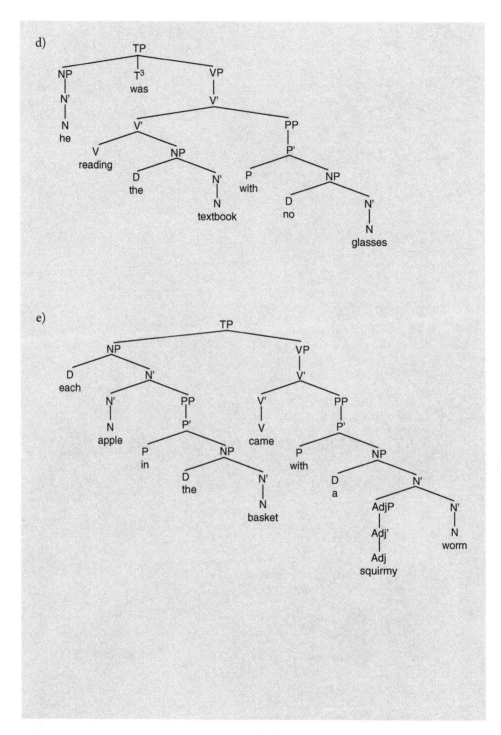

e)

f)

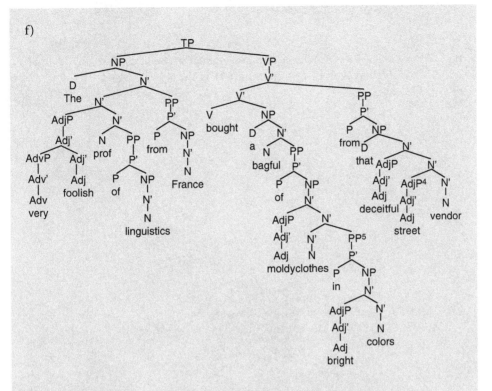

WBE10.   COMMON MISTAKES IN TREE DRAWING

a)   *Mistake 1:* The PP is drawn in as a specifier (on the right). It is daughter of NP and sister to N', which makes it an adjunct.
Mistake 2: The PP is missing the intermediate P' level.
The correct tree:

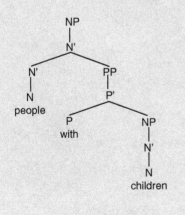

---

⁴ This could also be an NP and it could also be complement instead of an adjunct. It could even be treated as a compound noun: *street-vendor*. All of these analyses are possible.

⁵ This PP could also be attached higher than the AdjP headed by *moldy*.

b) *Mistake 1*: The PP *without a helmet* is an adjunct so should be sister to a V' level.
    Mistake 2: There is an extra, unnecessary N' in the NP.
     The correct tree:

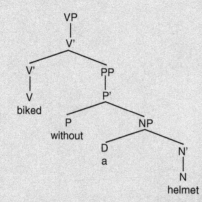

c) *Mistake 1*: The PP headed by *from* is missing the P'.
    Mistake 2: The PP *on Tuesday* modifies the verb *bought*, not the noun *store*.
     The correct tree:

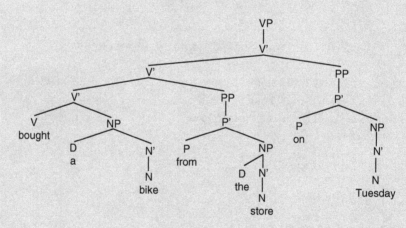

WBE11. JAPANESE PARAMETERS

1) *-o* marks objects, *-ga* marks subjects.
2) Subject Object Verb.
3) Complements precede their heads (the object precedes the verb).
4) Adjuncts precede their heads (adjectives precede the noun).
5) Specifiers precede their heads (determiners precede the noun).

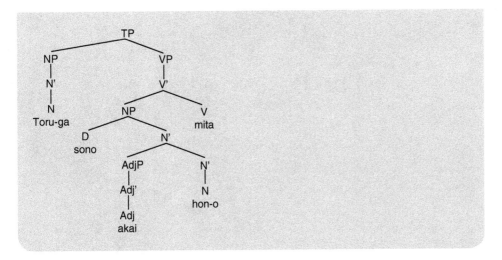

part 2

The Base

chapter 7

Extending X-bar Theory to Functional Categories

WORKBOOK EXERCISES

WBE1. GERMAN GENITIVE CASE
[Data Analysis; Basic]

Consider the following DP of German. NOM stands for Nominative case, GEN stands for genitive case, and MASC means masculine grammatical gender.

a) der   Titel des   Filmes
  the.NOM.MASC title the.GEN.MASC Film.GEN
  "the film's title/title of the film"

Is the German genitive construction more like the English *'s*-possessive or more like the English *of*-possessive? In what ways does it differ from each of the English constructions and in what ways is it the same?

 Using a DP structure, draw the tree for the sentence. Hint: In English *of*-possessives, the PP headed by *of* is a complement to the possessed noun.

The Syntax Workbook, First Edition. Andrew Carnie.
© 2013 Andrew Carnie. Published 2013 by John Wiley & Sons, Inc.

WBE2.   DP TREES
[Application of Skills; Basic]

Draw the trees for the following DPs.

a)   the stale meat
b)   the box of pencils
c)   Franklin's easy chair
d)   Keith's box of pencils
e)   the drunkenness of the woman's husband
f)   the woman's husband's drunkenness
g)   the smelly pile of Bill's socks
h)   the woman's husband's father's best friend's night of excessive drunken debauchery

WBE3.   SUBJECTS AND PREDICATE PHRASES
[Data Analysis; Basic]

In each of the sentences below, identify the subjects and the predicate phrases. Note that if a sentence has an embedded clause then it will have more than one subject and more than one predicate phrase.

a)   The lost city puzzled the intrepid explorer.
b)   I wonder if Heidi has served the bean salad.
c)   He came with the optimism that he would find the lost city of gold.
d)   Fawcett thought that Jack came to Brazil so that he could fulfill the prophecy of the Buddhist holy men.

WBE4.   SPECIFIER, COMPLEMENT, AND ADJUNCT CLAUSES
[Data Analysis; Intermediate/Advanced]

Determine if the embedded clauses in the following sentences are specifiers, complements, or adjuncts.

a)   I asserted that Teddy bought the statue so that he could scare his cousin.
b)   The appraiser was certain that the statue was a seventeenth-century replica.
c)   That prices keep going up frightens the president.

WBE5.   FINITE VS. NON-FINITE CLAUSES[1]
[Data Analysis; Basic]

Determine if the embedded clauses in the following sentences are finite or non-finite.

---

[1]   Some of the exercises in this chapter of the workbook are loosely based on those in Carnie (2011).

a)   I think that George left.
b)   I think that George should leave.
c)   I want George to leave.
d)   I believe George left.
e)   I believe George to have gone.
f)   I think George went to the store.
g)   I asked George to go to the store.
h)   I asked him to leave.
i)   I asked that he leave.
j)   I asked to leave.
k)   I saw him leave.
l)   Susan seems to have gone.
m)   It seems that Susan left.

WBE6.   THE PARTICLE *To*
[Critical Thinking; Intermediate]

In what ways is the *to* in infinitives like the preposition *to* in sentences like *I went to the store*, and in what ways is it different? Think carefully about what kinds of elements must follow the preposition *to* and what the meaning of the preposition *to* might be. Are these the same as the *to* in non-finite clauses?

WBE7.   WHAT CATEGORY IS *To*?
[Critical Thinking; Advanced]

In the main text, we called the infinitive marker *to* a T node. Your job in this exercise is to marshal some evidence that this is correct. Here are some things to think about: Modal verbs (which are the most prototypical instance of category T) consistently take the *bare* form of a verb (i.e., not a tensed form, a participial form, or a gerund):

1)   a)   Art will leave.
     b)   *Art will left.
     c)   *Art will leaves.
     d)   *Art will leaving.

What form of the verb follows infinitive *to*?
    Next think about the order of elements. Again compare *to* to modals:

2)   a)   Heidi will have eaten.
     b)   *Heidi have will eaten.
     c)   Heidi will be eating.
     d)   *Heidi is will eating/*Heidi be will eating.

Does *to* behave like a modal with respect to ordering? On these grounds give a short argument that *to* is a T node.

WBE8.   SPLIT INFINITIVES
[Critical Thinking; Advanced]

Part 1: In the sentence *Robert will boldly eat the chili-pepper*, what word does *boldly* modify? Is it a complement, adjunct, or specifier? Draw the tree for this sentence (assume chili-pepper is a compound noun).

Part 2: Now think about where *boldly* appears in the sentence *Bill wants Robert to boldly eat the chili-pepper*. Given your answer to part 1, where is the natural place to put *boldly* in the tree? Draw the tree for this sentence.

Part 3: One of the pet peeves of prescriptive grammarians is the so-called "split infinitive" such as the famous *To boldly go where no one has gone before*. In split infinitives, one finds an adverb (such as *boldly* in the famous sentence) between the *to* and the verb. The origins of this prescription are dubious at best – see for example the extensive discussion in Pinker (1995). In addition, one finds frequent examples of "split infinitives" in the works of many famous authors. Nevertheless, it is taught religiously in grammar classes around the world. Now given your answers to parts 1 and 2, what does this tell us about prescriptive grammar?

WBE9.   TREE DRAWING
[Data Analysis; Advanced]

Draw the trees for the following sentences:

a) Percy's obsessive love of the jungle began at a very young age.
b) The restaurant's unlabeled bottles of spices ensured that the spinach ice-cream had a funny aftertaste. *(Treat* had *as a main verb.)*
c) The crotchety linguist wanted you to transcribe those sentences into IPA before she left for supper. *(Treat* before *as a complementizer.)*

ANSWERS

WBE1.   GERMAN GENITIVE CASE

In terms of word order, it more closely resembles the *of*-possessive, because the item that is possessed comes first, followed by the possessor. It differs from the English *of*-possessive, however, in that there is no *of*-preposition, and that both the determiner and the possessor are marked with an *-s* suffix, reminiscent of the English *'s* (and perhaps cognate with it).

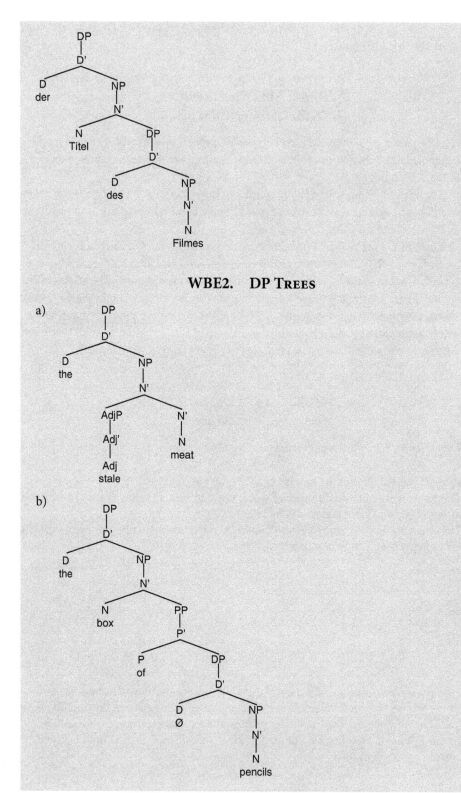

WBE2.   DP Trees

c)

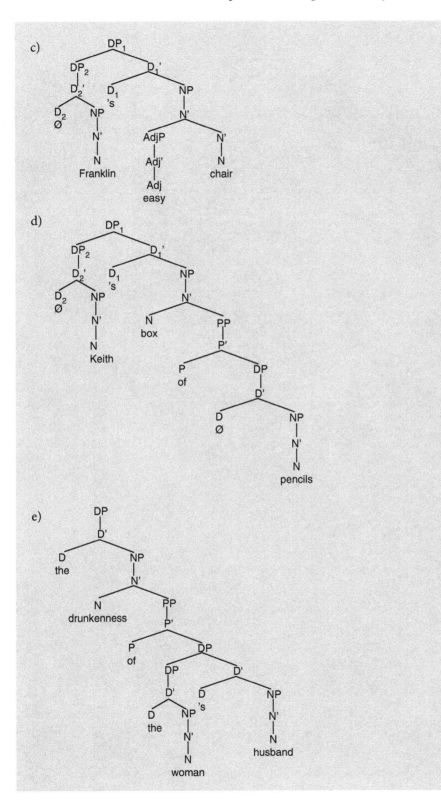

d)

e)

f)

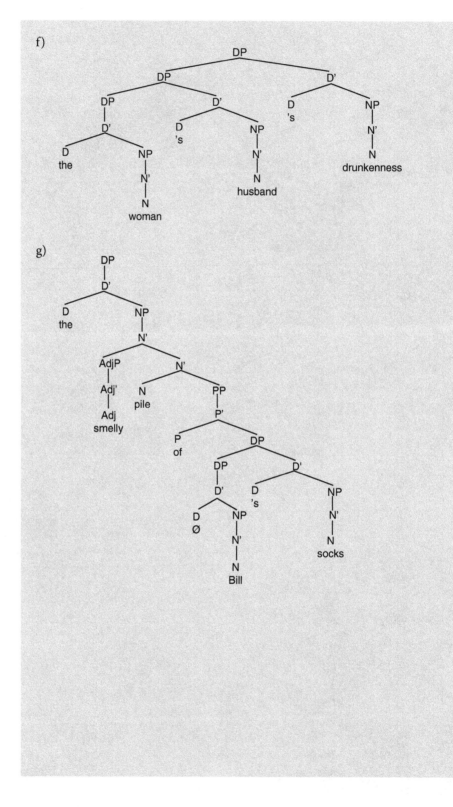

g)

h)

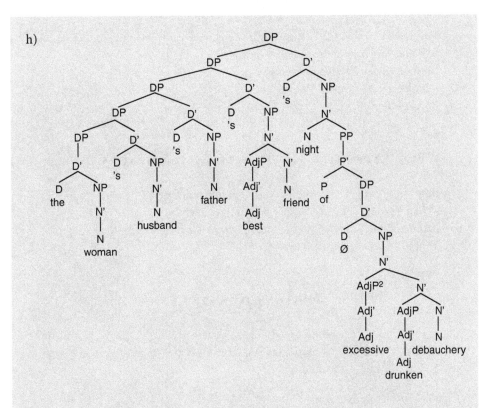

WBE3. SUBJECTS AND PREDICATE PHRASES

a)   Subject: *The lost city*
Predicate phrase: *puzzled the intrepid explorer*

b)   Main clause subject: *I*
Main clause predicate phrase: *wonder if Heidi has served the bean salad*
Embedded clause subject: *Heidi*
Embedded clause predicate phrase: *served the bean salad*

c)   Main clause subject: *He*
Main clause predicate phrase: *came with the optimism that he would find the lost city of gold*
Embedded clause subject: *he*
Embedded clause predicate phrase: *would find the lost city of gold*

d)   Main clause subject: *Fawcett*
Main clause predicate phrase: *thought that Jack came to Brazil so that he could fulfill the prophecy of the Buddhist holy men.*
Intermediate embedded clause subject: *Jack*

---

2   In this tree, I'm assuming that *excessive* modifies *debauchery*. I think that if *excessive* modified *drunken* it would be *excessively drunken* rather than *excessive* without the *-ly*.

Intermediate embedded clause predicate phrase: *came to Brazil so that he could fulfill the prophecy of the Buddhist holy men.*
Most deeply embedded clause subject: *he*
Most deeply embedded clause predicate phrase: *could fulfill the prophecy of the Buddhist holy men.*

WBE4.   Specifier, Complement, and Adjunct Clauses

a)   *that Teddy bought the statue* = complement to *asserted*
     so that he could scare his cousin = adjunct to *bought*
b)   *that the statue was a seventeenth-century replica* = complement to *certain*
c)   *That prices keep going up* = specifier of TP

WBE5.   Finite vs. Non-finite Clauses

a) finite   b) finite   c) non-finite   d) finite   e) non-finite   f) finite   g) non-finite
h) non-finite   i) finite   j) non-finite   k) non-finite (tricky because there is no *to* here)   l) non-finite   m) finite

WBE6.   The Particle *To*

The two words are pronounced alike, but that's where the similarities end. The preposition *to* must be followed by a DP (*I gave the book to the man, *I gave the book to red, *I gave the book to leave*). Non-finite *to* is always followed by a VP (*I want to leave, *I want to them*). They mean different things too. The preposition *to* marks DPs as being the goals or end points of actions; the *to* in non-finite sentences marks the lack of tense.

WBE7.   What Category Is *To*?

The non-finite marker *to* behaves in many ways like a modal. It appears before all other auxiliaries, and any verb that follows it has to be in its bare form. If modals are T categories, then it follows that so is *to*.

WBE8.   Split Infinitives

Part 1: The adverb *boldly* is an adjunct to the verb *eat*.
   I've drawn the tree here with full CP and TP structures, as argued for by the end of this chapter:

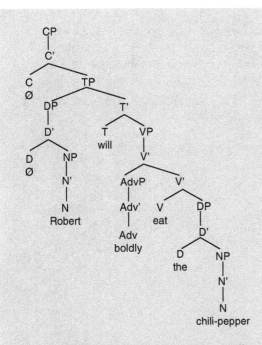

Part 2: If *boldly* is an adjunct to *eat*, it naturally occurs between the T head and the verb.

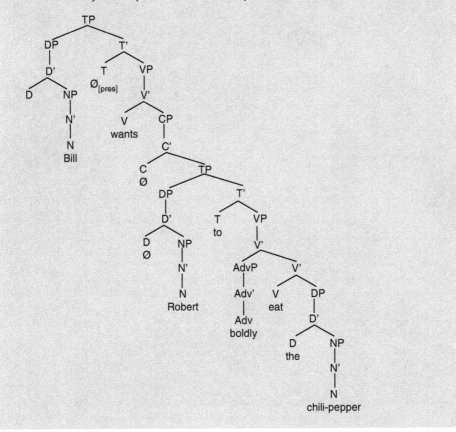

Part 3: X-bar theory predicts that the most natural place to adjoin an adverb like *boldly* is right between the *to* and the verb – the very place prescriptive grammarians forbid you to put it. Since X-bar theory has considerable explanatory power and the structures it predicts are pervasive in grammar, this suggests that we should ignore the prescriptivists on this point.

WBE9.   TREE DRAWING

a)

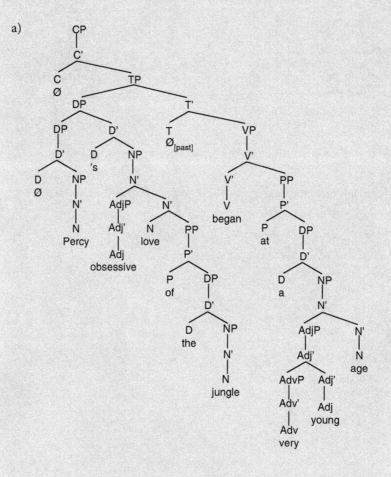

c)

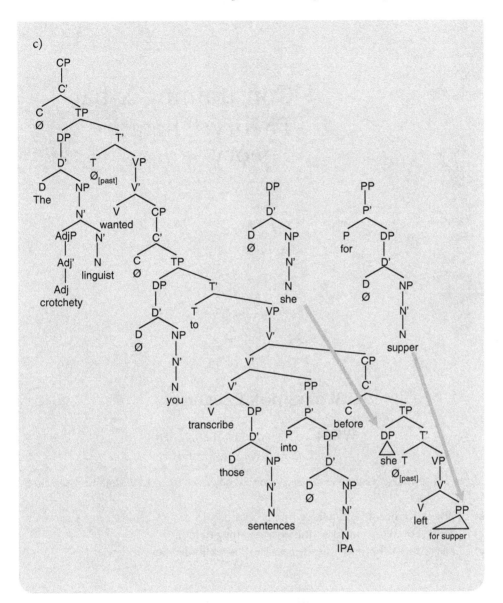

chapter 8

Constraining X-bar Theory: Theta Theory

WORKBOOK EXERCISES

WBE1.   THEMATIC RELATIONS
[Application of Knowledge; Basic]

Identify the thematic relations associated with each bracketed string in the following sentences.

a)   [Susan] overheard [Bill] talking [in the classroom].
b)   [Beth] shoved [the linguist] [into the oncoming traffic].
c)   [The boxer's father] got [prickly pear jam] [from his daughter-in-law].

WBE2.   YALARNNGA[1]
[Data Analysis; Basic]

Identify what the suffixes glossed as A, B, C, and D mean in Yalarnnga, a language spoken in Western Queensland, Australia. The glosses have been slightly simplified. Your answer should reference thematic relations.

---

[1]   Data from Breen and Blake (2007).

a) Mangurru-lu   tjala   tatja-mu   kaya-ka.
   dog-**A**   this   bite-past   child-**B**
   "The dog bit the child."

b) Tharntu-ngka   ninyi   ngathu   ngathi-mu   warri-ka.
   hole-**C**   here   1SG   cook-past   meat-**B**
   "I cooked the meat in this hole."

c) Kukapi-yangu   ngathu   miya-mu   kakuna
   grass-**D**   1SG   get-PAST   egg
   "I got the egg from the grass."

WBE3. FINNISH CASE AND THEMATIC RELATIONS[2]
[Data Analysis; Basic]

Finnish has a complex system of marking nouns. It has 15 different forms for each noun. These forms are known as cases. Some of the cases correspond to grammatical relations such as subject or object, but others seem to correspond to thematic relations. Here are four sentences with different forms of the Finnish word for "table"; what thematic relations do each of these forms correspond to?

a) Nähdään   talolla.
   see.you   house.ADESSIVE
   "See you at the house."

b) Kiersin   talolta   toiselle.
   toured.1s   house.ABLATIVE   another
   "I travelled from one house to another."

c) Koska   saavut   talolle?
   When   arrive   house.ALLATIVE
   "When will you be getting to the house?"

d) He   levittivät   sanomaansa   rakentaminensa   taloin.
   They spread   their.message   built   house.INSTRUCTIVE
   "They spread their message with the houses they built."

WBE4. ENGLISH OBJECT-DERIVED DEVERBAL ADJECTIVES[3]
[Data Analysis; Intermediate]

In English, it is possible to construct an adjective by taking an argument of the verb and prefixing it to an *-ing* form of the verb. So we can turn *the man loves peanuts* into *the peanut-loving man*. This process is quite productive, but it does have some restrictions.

---

[2] The data in this problem set was taken from the Wikipedia page on Finnish cases. Assistance with a previous version of this problem set was provided by Sakari Vaelma and Peter Slomanson, but they should not be held accountable for this version.

[3] Based on discussion in Farrell (1994), Grimshaw (1990), and Roeper (1987)

Observe the data in (1) where you can do this, and the data in (2) where you cannot. The examples are taken from Farrell (1994).

1)
   a) man-eating tigers
   b) god-fearing men
   c) fun-loving teenagers
   d) woman-chasing scoundrel
   e) thumb-sucking baby

2)
   a) *child-eating bread
   b) *baby-sucking thumb
   c) *teenager-loving fun

Couching your answer in terms of thematic relations, explain the difference between the adjectives in (1) and the adjectives in (2). Why can you create a compound like *man-eating tiger* and but not one like *child-eating bread*?

WBE5.   TWO KINDS OF INTRANSITIVES[4]
[Data Analysis; Intermediate]

Many languages express a morphological difference in the marking of subjects of intransitive clauses. One way to explain these data is to make reference to thematic relations. Consider the data below from Batsbi in (1), Choctaw in (2), and Lakhota in (3).

1) **Batsbi** (Nakh language family)
    a) So   wože.
        I.ABS fell
        "I fell."
    b) As   wože.
        I.ERG fell
        "I fell (my own fault)."

2) **Choctaw** (Muskogean family)
    a) Sa-ttola-tok.
        1.ACC-fall-past
        "I fell."
    b) Ittola-li-tok.
        fall-1-PAST
        "I fell on purpose."

3) **Lakhota**[5] (Siouan family)
    a) Ma-hîxpaye.
        1s-fall
        "I fell."

---

[4] The data from Batsbi is from Comrie (1973), the data from Choctaw comes from Davies (1981), and the data from Lakhota comes from Mithun (1991).

[5] Thanks to Kevin Schluter for pointing out these facts.

b) Wa-škate.
1s-play
"I play."

Don't worry too much about the ERG/ABS/ACC glosses on the subjects and don't worry about word/morpheme order, but think about the thematic relations each of the nouns in these sentences has. Can you describe in terms of thematic relations the difference between each of the (a) forms and each of the (b) forms of the subjects? The same explanation should work for all three languages.

WBE6. WESTERN VS. EASTERN BASQUE CASE[6]
[Data Analysis; Advanced]

Part 1, Western Basque: In Western dialects of Basque, the case marking on nouns seems to reflect thematic relations. Consider the data in (1)–(3) below. What thematic relation is associated with ergative case (ERG), and what thematic relation is associated with absolutive case (ABS)?

1) Peru-k   sagarr-a   jan   du.
   Peter-ERG apple-DET.ABS eaten has
   "Peter has eaten the apple."

2) Peru-k   dantzatu du.   (Western Basque only)
   Peter-ERG danced   has
   "Peter has danced."

3) Peru   erori   da.
   Peter-ABS fallen is
   "Peter has fallen."

Part 2, Eastern Basque: Eastern Basque has a different pattern:

4) Peru-k   sagarr-a   jan   du.
   Peter-ERG apple-DET.ABS eaten has
   "Peter has eaten the apple."

5) Peru   dantzatu da.   (Eastern Basque only)
   Peter.ABS danced   is
   "Peter has danced."

6) Peru   erori   da.
   Peter-ABS fallen is
   "Peter has fallen."

Can the pattern in Eastern Basque be explained using thematic relations? Why or why not?

---

[6]   Data from Aldai (2009) via a talk by Alice Harris at the 2011 Linguistic Society of America Summer Institute, July 19, Boulder, Colorado.

Part 3, Laz: Here is some data from Laz,[7] a language completely unrelated to Basque. (Laz is a Kartvelian language, Basque is a language isolate.) Does Laz behave more like Eastern or Western Basque in terms of marking its nouns for thematic relations?

7) Ǩoči-k   q'vilups γej-i.
    man-ERG   kill   pig-ABS
    "The man kills a pig."

8) Aya   ǩoči-k   ǩai   ibirs.
    this man-ERG   well sing
    "This man sings well."

9) Ǩoči   γurun.
    man.ABS   dies
    "The man dies."

WBE7.   TAGALOG
[Data Analysis; Advanced]

In Tagalog (and many other Austronesian languages as well), verbs can take three different forms. To avoid biasing the situation, we've glossed these three forms as A, T, and L. These three forms differ in what is the "topic" of the sentence (i.e., what the sentence is about). The topic itself is marked with the determiner *ang* (don't confuse *ang* with *ng*!). Using the limited data below, and making direct reference to thematic relations, can you describe when each of the different verbs forms (A, T, L) is used? (Data from Payne 1997, p. 54; glosses slightly modified.)

a) Humiram   ang   babae   ng   pera   sa   bangko.
    borrow.A   the.TOPIC   woman   the   money   OBL   bank
    "The woman borrowed the money from a bank."

b) Hiniram   ng   babae   ang   pera   sa   bangko.
    borrow.T   the   woman   the.TOPIC   money   OBL   bank
    "It was the money that the woman borrowed from a bank."

c) Hiniraman   ng   babae   sa   pera   ang   bangko.
    Borrow.L   the   woman   OBL   money   the.TOPIC   bank
    "It was from a bank that the woman borrowed the money."

WBE8.   THETA GRIDS
[Application of Skills, Data Analysis; Basic]

Draw the theta grids for each of the verbs in the following sentences. Remember that adjuncts are not included in theta grids.

---

7   Data also from Harris (2011).

a) Louis loved some cookies with his coffee.
b) Heidi sent a cake to Art on his birthday.
c) The book arrived with a note.
d) Josh parked his car next to the fire hydrant.

WBE9. THETA CRITERION
[Application of Skills, Data Analysis; Basic]

All of the following sentences are violations of the Theta Criterion. Identify what DP (or lack thereof) is creating the problem and how it creates a violation of the Theta Criterion.

a) *Calvin bought Andrew a statue a painting.
b) *Calvin rains.
c) *Louis loves.
d) #The spinach ice-cream despised jalapeno-flavored hard candy.

WBE10. NOT ALL *ITS* ARE CREATED EQUAL
[Application of Knowledge; Basic]

There are two types of the pronoun *it* in English. One can be assigned a theta role and refer to some non-human object; the other can be an expletive. Identify if the *its* in the following sentences are expletives without theta roles or pronouns with theta roles.

a) It is muggy out there.
b) It fell on Kevin's head.
c) It seems that Art made peppermint-flavored turkey pie.
d) It ran past me on the road.
e) I love it!
f) It was really boring.
g) It appears that Pangur lost his toy.

ANSWERS

WBE1. THEMATIC RELATIONS

a) [*Susan*] = experiencer; [*Bill*] = agent; [*in the classroom*] = location.
b) [*Beth*] = agent; [*the linguist*] = theme; [*into the oncoming traffic*] = either location or goal.
c) [*The boxer's father*] = recipient; [*prickly pear jam*] = theme; [*from his daughter-in-law*] = source.

WBE2.   Yalarnnga

A = Agent; B = theme; C = Location; D = source.

WBE3.   Finnish Case and Thematic Relations

a)   adessive = location
b)   ablative = source
c)   allative = goal
d)   instructive = instrument

WBE4.   English Object-derived Deverbal Adjectives

The first noun can be a theme and the second an agent, but not vice versa.

WBE5.   Two Kinds of Intransitives

The (a) forms have either theme (or perhaps experiencer) subjects. The (b) forms all have agent subjects.

WBE6.   Western vs. Eastern Basque Case

Part 1, Western Basque: Ergative marks agents, Absolutive marks themes.
Part 2, Eastern Basque: No, Eastern Basque case marking can't be accounted for using thematic relations, because both the agent in the (a) sentence and the agent in the (b) sentence are marked with different cases. And the (b) and (c) sentences, which have different thematic relations on the subject, are marked with the same case. Eastern Basque has what is traditionally viewed as an ergative/absolutive case pattern, where the objects of transitives and the subjects of all intransitives are marked with absolutive and the subjects of transitives are marked with ergative. The case marking pays attention to grammatical relations rather than thematic relations.
Part 3, Laz: Laz behaves like Western Basque.

WBE7.   Tagalog

The A form is used when the topic is an agent, the T form is used when the topic is a theme, and the L form is used when the topic is a location of some sort (in the examples given, the L form is used with a source).

WBE8.   THETA GRIDS

Draw the theta grids for each of the verbs in the following sentences. Remember that adjuncts are not included in theta grids.

a)   Louis$_i$ desired [some cookies]$_k$ with his coffee.

desire

Experiencer DP	Theme DP
i	k

[with his coffee] is an adjunct so isn't included in the theta grid.

b)   Heidi$_i$ sent [a cake]$_k$ [to Art]$_m$ on his birthday.

send

Agent / Source DP	Theme DP	Goal PP
i	k	m

[on his birthday] is an adjunct so isn't included in the theta grid.

c)   [The book]$_i$ arrived with a note.

arrive

Theme DP
i

[With a note] is an adjunct and isn't included in the theta grid. *Arrive* is a very tricky verb because the subject is a theme rather than an agent.

d) Josh$_i$ parked [his car]$_k$ next to the fire hydrant.

parked

<u>Agent</u> DP	Theme DP
i	k

[next to the fire hydrant] is an adjunct.

WBE9.   THETA CRITERION

a) This sentence has two DPs filling the theme theta role: [*a statue*] and [*a painting*].
b) The verb *rain* doesn't allow any DPs with theta roles, only an expletive, so *Calvin* doesn't have a theta role.
c) *Love* requires a theme, which is missing from this sentence.
d) Technically speaking this isn't a violation of the Theta Criterion, which as formulated in the text doesn't require a match to the thematic relation in the theta grid, only a match in the number of arguments. However, we can assume *despise* requires a possible experiencer and *the spinach ice-crea*m doesn't seem like a likely candidate as an experiencer.

WBE10.   NOT ALL *ITS* ARE CREATED EQUAL

a) expletive   b) pronoun with a theta role   c) expletive   d) pronoun with a theta role   e)   pronoun with a theta role   f)   pronoun with a theta role   g)   expletive

Auxiliaries and Functional Categories

chapter 9

Workbook Exercises

WBE1. Categorizing Verbs
[Data Analysis; Intermediate/Advanced]

Part 1: Assign acceptability judgments to the following sentences. If you aren't a native speaker, ask a native speaker friend to help you.

1) a) I believed that you saw a UFO.
    b) I believed you saw a UFO.
    c) I believed if you saw a UFO.
    d) I believed you to have seen a UFO.
    e) I believe to have seen a UFO.

2) a) Heidi and I discussed that the outcome of the election was unexpected. (Note: do *not* mentally insert a "the fact" in the middle of this sentence!)
    b) Heidi and I discussed the outcome of the election was unexpected.
    c) Heidi and I discussed if/whether the outcome of the election was unexpected.

The Syntax Workbook, First Edition. Andrew Carnie.
© 2013 Andrew Carnie. Published 2013 by John Wiley & Sons, Inc.

    d)   Heidi and I discussed the outcome of the election to be unexpected.

    e)   Heidi and I discussed to leave immediately.

3)   a)   Art demanded that we go to the local brewpub.

    b)   Art demanded we go to the local brewpub.

    c)   Art demanded if we go to the local brewpub.

    d)   Art demanded us to go to the local brewpub.

    e)   Art demanded to go to the local brewpub.

4)   a)   Andy wondered that we should go.

    b)   Andy wondered we should go.

    c)   Andy wondered if we should go.

    d)   Andy wondered us to go.

    e)   Andy wondered to go home.

Part 2: Based on your judgments above, draw the theta grids for *believe*, *discuss*, *demand*, and *wonder*. Use the following principles for deciding whether to use [+Q] or [–Q], or leave [±Q] unspecified:

- Assign [+Q] if both (a) and (b) are unacceptable, but (c) is acceptable.
- Assign [–Q] if either of (a) or (b) or both is acceptable, but (c) is unacceptable.
- Don't assign any value if either of (a) or (b) are acceptable and (c) is acceptable as well.

Then use the following principles for deciding whether to use [+FINITE] or [–FINITE], or leave the verb unspecified for [±FINITE]:

- Assign [–FINITE] if all of (a), (b), and (c) are ungrammatical, but either of (d) or (e) is acceptable.
- Assign [+FINITE] if any of (a), (b), or (c) are grammatical and both (d) and (e) are unacceptable.
- Don't assign any value for [±FINITE] if at least one of (a), (b), and (c) is acceptable, and either (c) or (d) is acceptable.

Some of these verbs can take DPs as well as CPs as complements; ignore that fact in your theta grids (but do put the DP external arguments in).

WBE2. Selection by Complementizers
[Data Analysis; Basic]

Draw the theta grids for the following complementizers used in the following sentences, referencing the feature [±INFINITIVE]:

a)   I saw he was here.
b)   I want him to leave.
c)   I asked for John to find a new workstation.

WBE3.   *This and That*
[Application of Knowledge; Basic]

Draw the theta grids for the determiners *that* and *this*.

WBE4.   **French Determiners**
[Data Analysis; Basic]

Background: Nouns in French are divided up into two genders or noun classes. The gender actually has little or nothing to do with the sex of the item described by the noun, as all inanimate and sexless objects are also given a gender. The two genders in French are called **masculine** and **feminine**. We can represent this distinction with the feature [±FEMININE], where [−FEMININE] is taken to represent the masculine noun class. For most nouns the assignment of this feature is arbitrary and must be memorized when learning the language. For example, the nouns *chaise* 'chair' and *maison* 'house' are feminine, and the nouns *livre* 'book' and *câble* 'cable' are masculine.

Part 1: There are different determiners for masculine and feminine nouns. Draw the theta grids for *un*, *une*, *le*, and *la*, based on the data below. Assume that like *the* and *a* in English, these determiners require [+COUNT] nouns.

a)   une chaise   'a chair'
b)   une maison   'a house'
c)   un livre   'a book'
d)   un câble   'a cable'
e)   la chaise   'the chair'
f)   la maison   'the house'
g)   le livre   'the book'
h)   le câble   'the cable'
i)   *la chaises   'the chairs'
j)   *le livres   'the chairs'
k)   *la Marie   'the Mary'
l)   *le Pierre   'the Peter'
m) *la elle   'the she'
n)   *le il   'the he'

Part 2: French has another determiner, *les*, which is seen in (o–r). Draw the theta grid for this determiner. Does it require specification for the feature [±FEMININE]?

o)   les chaises   'the chairs'
p)   les maisons   'the houses'
q)   les livres   'the books'
r)   les câbles   'the cables'

WBE5.   Tense
[Data Analysis; Basic]

Identify whether the following sentences are in the past, present or future:

a)   The parakeet flew home.
b)   Calvin loves snow cones.
c)   Otto drank the tuna juice.
d)   Reggie will wake everyone up.
e)   Andrew brushed the cat.
f)   I drink too much.
g)   Sylvia was smoking in the boys' room.
h)   Jeff had eaten the deep-fried English muffins.
i)   Mike is writing a love poem in Welsh.

WBE6.   Perfect
[Data Analysis; Basic]

The following paragraph contains three sentences in the perfect aspect. What are they?

I was driving into Tucson to buy some tortillas, when I noticed that my car was nearly out of gas. I was surprised because I had filled the tank yesterday. I have driven all over town. However, I hadn't gone that far.

WBE7.   Perfect and Tense Combined
[Data Analysis; Basic]

Identify the aspect and tense of each of the following sentences. Be especially careful about the present perfect, which sometimes feels a bit like a past. You can identify the present perfect by virtue of the fact that the verb *have* is either in its *have* form (with no *will* before it!) or in its *has* form.

a)   Susan has danced already.
b)   Calvin will have slept all day.
c)   Heidi danced yesterday.
d)   Art had danced already.
e)   Calvin will sleep all day.

f)   Art drinks whisky sours.
g)   Dave will drink a whisky sour.
h)   Dan had drunk a whisky sour.
i)   I have never eaten beef waffles.

WBE8.   ASPECT AND TENSE COMBINED
[Data Analysis; Intermediate]

Identify the aspect and tense of each of the following sentences.

a)   Calvin is sleeping on top of the fridge.
b)   Otto grabbed at the passing stick.
c)   Heidi will be grading her papers.
d)   Art has pulled down the outer wall.
e)   Andrew will eat the beef waffles.
f)   Jean was driving to her daughter's house.
g)   Jean had driven to her daughter's house.

WBE9.   VOICE
[Data Analysis; Basic]

Identify which of the following sentences are active and which are passive:

a)   Calvin caught the mouse.
b)   The retaining wall was torn down.
c)   Otto drank the tuna juice.
d)   Dave played the game.
e)   Art tore down the retaining wall.
f)   The game will be played.

WBE10.   VOICE, ASPECT, AND TENSE COMBINED
[Data Analysis; Basic]

For each sentence below, identify if it is present, past, or future; if it is perfect or not; if it's progressive or non-progressive; and whether it is active or passive.

a)   Pangur was being massaged.
b)   Surrey will have been adopted.
c)   Calvin is eating the tuna.
d)   The tuna has been eaten.
e)   Calvin has been eating the tuna.
f)   The wall had been torn down.

WBE11.   MODALS
[Critical Thinking; Basic]

The auxiliary *is* can appear before negation as in *He is not eating the muffins*. Is this evidence that the verb *be* is a modal or not? Explain your answer.

WBE12.   MAIN VERBS VS. AUXILIARIES
[Data Analysis; Basic]

Identify whether the inflected forms of the verbs *do, have,* and *be* in the following sentences are main verbs or auxiliaries.

a)   I am a student of linguistics.
b)   I am running for office.
c)   I have a bowl of peanuts in my office.
d)   I have eaten a bowl of peanuts.
e)   I do not have a bowl of peanuts.
f)   I did everything that you asked me to.

WBE13.   MODAL COMPLEMENTS
[Application of Skills; Basic]

Draw the theta grid for *will*.

WBE14.   PRESENT TENSE T
[Application of Skills; Basic]

Draw the theta grid for $\emptyset_{pres}$.

WBE15.   PAST PERFECT PASSIVE
[Application of Skills; Basic]

Draw the tree for the sentence *The tuna had been eaten*. Don't worry about the fact that *the tuna* is a theme, just put it in subject position anyway.

WBE16.   PAST PROGRESSIVE
[Application of Skills; Basic]

Draw the tree for the sentence *The cat was leaving*.

ANSWERS

WBE1. CATEGORIZING VERBS

Part 1: The following are my judgments. Yours may very well differ:

1) a) I believed that you saw a UFO.
   b) I believed you saw a UFO.
   c) *I believed if you saw a UFO.
   d) I believed you to have seen a UFO.
   e) *I believe to have seen a UFO

2) a) *?Heidi and I discussed that the outcome of the election was unexpected.
   b) *Heidi and I discussed the outcome of the election was unexpected.
   c) Heidi and I discussed if/whether the outcome of the election was unexpected.
   d) *Heidi and I discussed the outcome of the election to be unexpected.
   e) *Heidi and I discussed to leave immediately

Note: There are many people who seem to accept sentence (2a). This will change your answer to the theta grid portion of this question below.

3) a) Art demanded that we go to the local brewpub.
   b) Art demanded we go to the local brewpub.
   c) *Art demanded if we go to the local brewpub.
   d) *Art demanded us to go to the local brewpub.
   e) Art demanded to go to the local brewpub.

4) a) *Andy wondered that we should go.
   b) *Andy wondered we should go.
   c) Andy wondered if we should go.
   d) *Andy wondered us to go.
   e) *Andy wondered to go home.

Note: There are many people who seem to accept sentence (4a). This will change your answer to the theta grid portion of this question below.

Part 2:
believe: For me, the verb *believe* has the following theta grid:

believed

Experiencer	CP
DP	[–Q]

We know that the embedded CP must be [–Q] because it does not allow *if* complements (1c), but does allow *that* and Ø complements (1a and 1b). *Believe* can take both
finite (1a) and non-finite complement clauses (1d) (although it can't take a subjectless
one as in 1e). Since it can take either finite or non-finite complement clauses, we leave
the feature [±FINITE] unspecified in the theta grid.

discuss: In my dialect of English, *discussed* has the following theta grid:

discussed

Agent	CP
DP	[+Q, +FINITE]

We know that *discuss* takes a [+FINITE] CP complement because sentence (2c) is
acceptable and both (2d) and (2e) are not. More controversial is the status of the [±Q]
feature. If you agree with me that sentence (2a) is ungrammatical, then this has to be
a [+Q], as in the theta grid above. Of course if you are one of the people who find (2a)
okay, then the [±Q] feature would be unspecified, and absent from the grid.

demand: Assuming judgments similar to mine, *demand* has the following theta
grid:

demand

Agent	CP
DP	[–Q]

This verb doesn't allow CP complements headed by *if*, so it must be [–Q]. But since
both (3a) and (3e) are acceptable, we don't specify the feature [±FINITE].

wonder: *Wonder* is identical to *discuss*.

WBE2.   SELECTION BY COMPLEMENTIZERS

a)

$\emptyset_{\text{[+finite]}}$

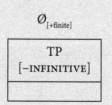

TP
[–INFINITIVE]

b)

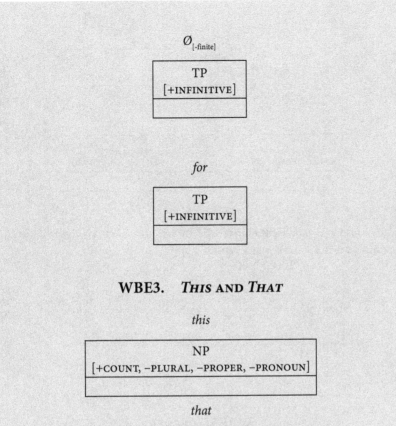

$\emptyset_{[\text{-finite}]}$

TP
[+INFINITIVE]

c)

for

TP
[+INFINITIVE]

WBE3.   *THIS AND THAT*

this

NP
[+COUNT, −PLURAL, −PROPER, −PRONOUN]

that

NP
[+COUNT, −PLURAL, −PROPER, −PRONOUN]

WBE4.   FRENCH DETERMINERS

Part 1:

un

NP
[−FEMININE, +COUNT, −PLURAL, −PROPER, −PRONOUN]

une

NP
[+FEMININE, +COUNT, −PLURAL, −PROPER, −PRONOUN]

le

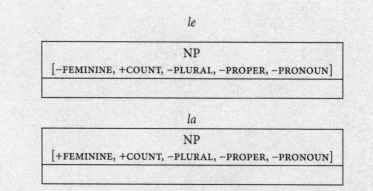

$$[-\text{FEMININE}, +\text{COUNT}, -\text{PLURAL}, -\text{PROPER}, -\text{PRONOUN}]$$

la

$$[+\text{FEMININE}, +\text{COUNT}, -\text{PLURAL}, -\text{PROPER}, -\text{PRONOUN}]$$

Part 2: Because *les* can take either masculine or feminine nouns it doesn't have any specification for the feature [±FEMININE].

les

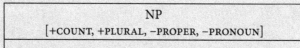

$$[+\text{COUNT}, +\text{PLURAL}, -\text{PROPER}, -\text{PRONOUN}]$$

WBE5.   TENSE

a) past   b) present   c) past,   d) future   e) past
f) present   g) past   h) past   i) present.

WBE6.   PERFECT ASPECT

I had filled the tank; I had driven all over town; I hadn't gone that far.

WBE7.   PERFECT AND TENSE COMBINED

a)   present perfect   b) future perfect   c) past non-perfect
d)   past perfect   e) future non-perfect   f) present non-perfect
g)   future non-perfect   h) past perfect   i) present perfect

WBE8.   ASPECT AND TENSE COMBINED

a)   present progressive   b)   past non-perfect/non-progressive
c)   future progressive   d)   present perfect   e)   future non-perfect/
non-progressive   f)   past progressive   g)   past perfect

WBE9.   VOICE

a)   active   b)   passive   c)   active   d)   active   e)   active
f)   passive

WBE10.   VOICE, ASPECT, AND TENSE COMBINED

a)   past non-perfect progressive passive   b)   future perfect non-progressive
passive   c)   present non-perfect progressive active   d)   present perfect
non-progressive passive   e)   present perfect progressive active   f)   past
perfect non-progressive passive

WBE11.   MODALS

Although the *is* in *He is not eating muffins* precedes negation, this is not evidence that
be is a modal. *Be* can also follow negation, as in *He has not been eating*. This example
also shows that *be* can follow other modals. Finally, *is* agrees with the third person
subject; agreement is a behavior that modals don't show.

WBE12.   MAIN VERBS VS. AUXILIARIES

a)   *be*$_{cop}$ (main verb)
b)   *be*$_{prog}$ (auxiliary)
c)   *have*$_{poss}$ (main verb)
d)   *have*$_{perf}$ (auxiliary)
e)   *do*$_{aux}$ (auxiliary) and *have*$_{poss}$ (main verb)
f)   *do*$_{main}$ (main verb)

WBE13. MODAL COMPLEMENTS

will

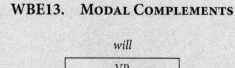

All modals in English will have a theta grid like the one above.

WBE14. PRESENT TENSE T

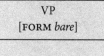

WBE15. PAST PERFECT PASSIVE

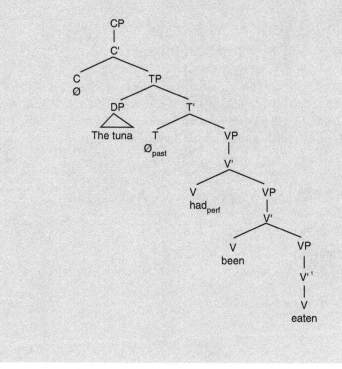

---

¹ Note that *tuna* actually starts as the complement of *eat*. We will address the movement in chapter 11.

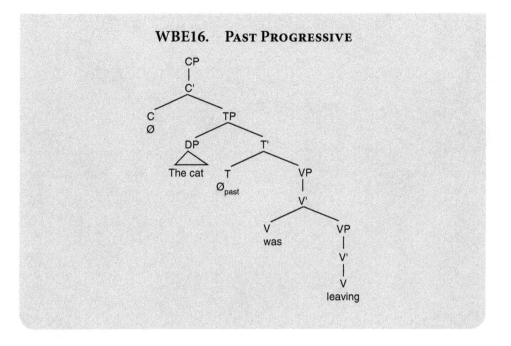

WBE16.   PAST PROGRESSIVE

chapter 10

Head-to-Head Movement

WORKBOOK EXERCISES

WBE1. VARDAR MACEDONIAN[1]
[Data Analysis; Intermediate]

The Vardar Macedonian language has three ways of forming yes/no questions: (1) you can simply add rising intonation, (2) you can do subject–verb inversion, or (3) you can use a question particle.

1) Teo   sviri   klavir?
    Teo   play.3s   piano.def
    "Does Teo play the piano?"

2) Sviri   Teo   klavir?
    play.3s   Teo   piano.def
    "Does Teo play the piano?"

3) Dali   Steve   zivee   vo   London?
    Q   Steve   live.3s   in   London
    "Does Steve live in London?"

---

[1] Data from Lazarova-Nikovska (2003).

The Syntax Workbook, First Edition. Andrew Carnie.
© 2013 Andrew Carnie. Published 2013 by John Wiley & Sons, Inc.

We will ignore the intonational mechanism here and concentrate on (2) and (3). On the basis of this data does Vardar Macedonian have V to T movement of main verbs or not? Why, or why not?

WBE2.   Mezquital Otomí[2]
[Data Analysis; Basic]

From the word order in the single Mezquital Otomí sentence below can you tell if the language is V → T or not?

Da-bëtsʔi   ri   tsïntʔi   mãɲã   ri   fani.
FUT.climb   2s   boy   onto   2s   horse
"Your boy will climb onto your horse."

WBE3.   Urim[3]
[Data Analysis; Basic]

On the basis of the following three sentences determine if Urim has V → T. Assume that *wet* is an auxiliary meaning "just happened", glossed here as REC for recent, and assume that *mpa* is an auxiliary verb meaning future, glossed here as FUT.

1) Kupm   antam   namu.
   1s   boil   plantain
   "I boil plantains/I am boiling plantains."

2) Wet   kupm   antam   namu.
   REC   1s   boil   plantain
   "I just boiled plantains."

3) Mpa   kupm   intam   namu.
   FUT   1s   boil   plantain
   "I will boil plantains."

Bonus challenge: Try drawing the trees for these sentences. You will need to use VP-internal subjects to make it work.

WBE4.   SOV Order and Verb Raising?
[Critical Thinking; Advanced]

In Subject-Object-Verb (SOV) order languages like Japanese, the verb appears at the end of the sentence, followed by any auxiliaries and complementizers. All adjuncts appear before the verb. It is very difficult to determine if there has been any verb raising or not. Explain why.

---

[2]   Data selected from Merriman et al. (2003: 168).

[3]   Data selected from Merriman et al. (2003: 229). Glosses have been slightly adjusted for pedagogical purposes.

WBE5. ENGLISH TREE DRAWING

[Application of Skills; Basic]

Draw the trees for the following English sentences. Be sure to indicate any auxiliary verb movement. Also don't forget about VP-internal subjects!

a) Art often goes to the movies.
b) Has Heidi lost her book-bag again?
c) Alex does not know anything about sausage making.

WBE6. FRENCH TREE DRAWING

[Application of Skills; Basic]

Draw the trees for the following French sentences. Be sure to indicate any verb movement. Also don't forget about VP-internal subjects!

a) Patrice   n'a   pas   marché   jusqu'à   l'   école.
    Patrice   has   not   walked   to   the   school.
    "Patrice hasn't walked to the school." (For the purposes of this tree, treat *n'a* as one word and ignore the negative part of it.)

b) Avez-   vous   vu   Patrice?
    Have   you   seen   Patrice?
    "Have you seen Patrice?"

c) Patrice   oublie   souvent   ses   chaussures
    Patrice   forgets   often   his   shoes
    "Patrice often forgets his shoes."

ANSWERS

WBE1. VARDAR MACEDONIAN

The alternation between the initial verb in (2) and the question particle in (3), where the main verb shifts in position relative to the subject, demonstrates that Vardar Macedonian allows main verbs to undergo $T \rightarrow C$ movement. This in turn entails that the V has raised via $V \rightarrow T$ movement to allow it to undergo to the subsequent movement to initial position.

WBE2.   Mezquital Otomí

The data here is extremely limited, but assuming that it's representative, Otomí is a VSO language, like Irish. Since the subject appears between the verb and its complement, it's reasonable to claim that the language has V → T movement around the subject.

WBE3.   Urim

In this data, we have evidence that the verb doesn't undergo V → T. The main verb always follows the subject and never appears in the same position as auxiliaries. The additional twist here is that the subject follows the auxiliary, which means it has to have VP-internal subjects.

(1)

(2)

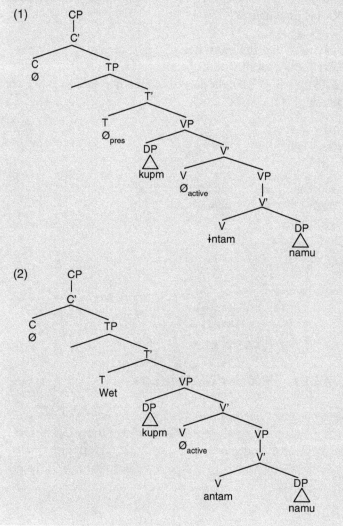

(3)

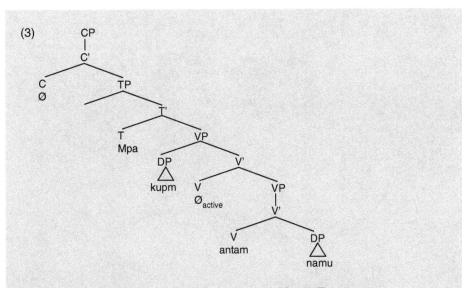

WBE4. SOV Order and Verb Raising?

It's either impossible or very difficult to tell if head-final languages have verb movement or not, because the V, T, and C are all lined up on the right edge, and one can't put any intervening landmark material such as negation, adverbs, etc. between them.

WBE5. English Tree Drawing

a) I'm leaving off the internal structure of DPs and PPs here, representing them with triangles, but these DPs and PPs will look just like ones we've seen earlier in the workbook.

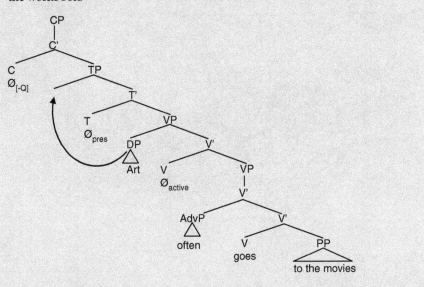

(b)

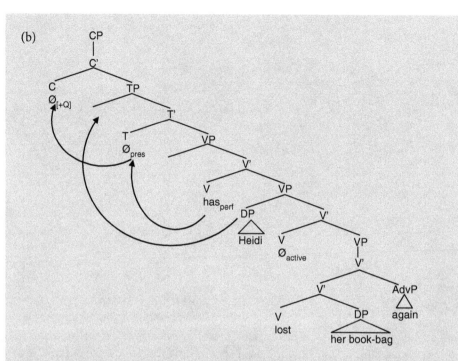

One tricky property of this tree is that the order of elements in the D-structure is the same as the order of elements in the S-structure (i.e., both the D-structure and the S-structure have the order *Has Heidi lost her book-bag again*). But theory-internal reasons force us to claim that there is V → T movement of the auxiliary, T → C movement to form a question and the DP moves from its VP-internal position to the specifier of TP, like all other subjects in English.

(c)

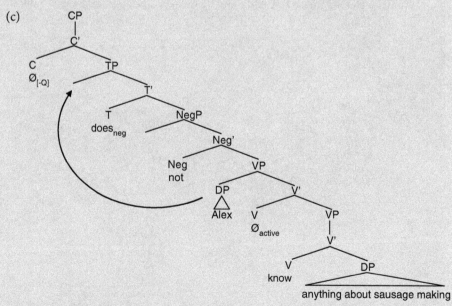

This sentence uses *do*-support because of the negative *not*.

WBE6.   FRENCH TREE DRAWING

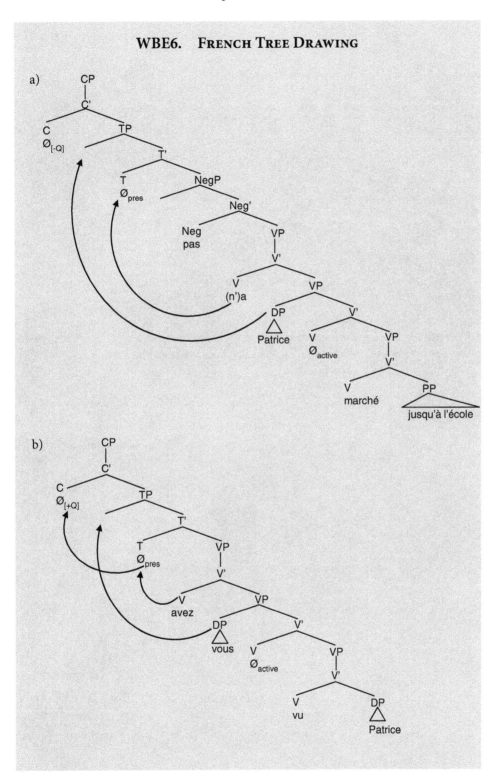

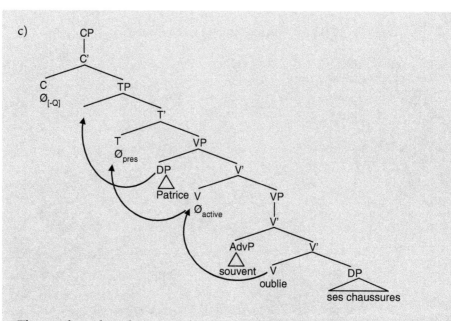

The extra hop where the main verb stops in $\emptyset_{active}$ before moving on to T is motivated by a constraint we'll look at in chapter 12, called the Minimal Link Condition (MLC).

part 3

Movement

chapter 11

DP Movement

WORKBOOK EXERCISES

WBE1. RAISING VERBS
[Data Analysis; Basic]

Which of the following main clause verbs (bold-faced in the sentences below) have agent theta roles and which have the subject of the embedded clause raised into subject position?

a)   Dan **seems** to have eaten mushrooms à la mode.
b)   Dan **wants** to have eaten mushrooms à la mode.
c)   Dan **is eager** to eat mushrooms à la mode.
d)   Dan **is certain** to have eaten mushrooms à la mode.

WBE2. TREES
[Applications of Skills; Intermediate]

Draw the D-structure trees for the sentences (a) and (d) in WBE1 above. Be explicit about what transformations derived the S-structure tree (if any). Recall that we have the following transformations: Expletive insertion, DP movement (both raising and passive), verb movement, T → C movement, and *do*-support/insertion. Annotate the D-structure tree

The Syntax Workbook, First Edition. Andrew Carnie.
© 2013 Andrew Carnie. Published 2013 by John Wiley & Sons, Inc.

with arrows to show the derivation of the S-structure. You can treat *mushrooms à la mode* as a compound noun.

WBE3.   PASSIVES AND ACTIVES
[Data Analysis; Basic]

Identify which of the following verbs are passive and which are active.

a)   Pangur ate the tuna.
b)   Drywall was put up just before the holidays.
c)   Thomas drank the milk.
d)   Jennifer smelled the milk.
e)   Art put up the drywall.
f)   The piano will be played.

WBE4.   TREES II
[Applications of Skills; Intermediate]

Draw the trees for sentences (a) and (f) in WBE3 above.

WBE5.   CASE
[Applications of Skills; Basic]

Identify how each DP in the following sentences checks Case.

a)   Heidi left the airport at midnight.
b)   Jean should travel to Ecuador.
c)   She thinks that Damian will eat the mushrooms in chocolate sauce.
d)   The book seems to have been written in French.
e)   Lionel seems to have written a book in French.
f)   Fiona has been contradicted by Theresa.
g)   The award was given to the best presentation at the conference.
h)   Morag began to eat cheese.
i)   The cheese was eaten by the mouse.

WBE6.   TREES III
[Applications of Skills; Basic]

Draw the trees for the sentences (b), (d), and (i) in WBE5. Be sure to indicate all movements with arrows.

WBE7. Irish Passive[1]
[Data Analysis; Advanced]

Modern Irish marks its passive with a special verb form, called the "autonomous" form in traditional grammars of the language. An active sentence is seen in (a). A grammatical passive is seen in (b).

a) Bhuail   Gaillimh   iad   sa   gcluife   deireanach.
    Beat.PAST   Galway   them.ACC   in.the   game   last
    "Galway beat them in the last game."

b) Buaileadh   iad   sa   gcluife   deireanach.
    beat.PAST.PASS   them.ACC   in.the   game   last
    "They were beaten in the last game."

Part 1: The Irish passive differs in two critical ways from the English passive. What are they?
Part 2: How can you encode the fact that the object of the passive in Irish takes the accusative case in our system?
Part 3 (advanced): Draw the trees for (a) and (b).

Answers

WBE1. Raising Verbs

Seem and *is certain* (a and c) are raising predicates. The agent is not assigned as part of the matrix subject. *Want* and *is eager* are what are called control predicates, which we'll address in chapter 15.

---

[1]   The data is based on and slightly modified from Stenson (1989).

WBE2. Trees

a)

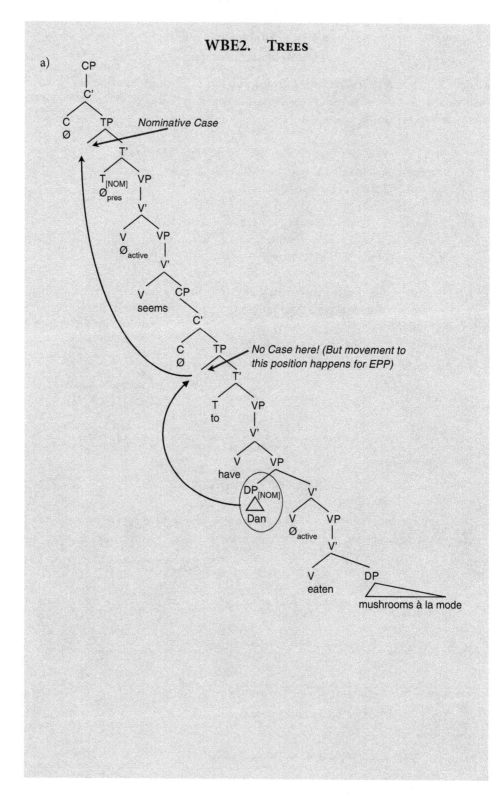

d)

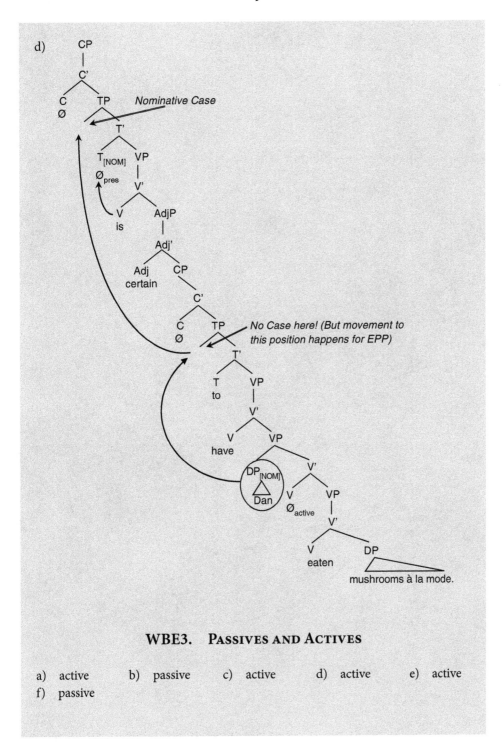

WBE3. Passives and Actives

a) active   b) passive   c) active   d) active   e) active
f) passive

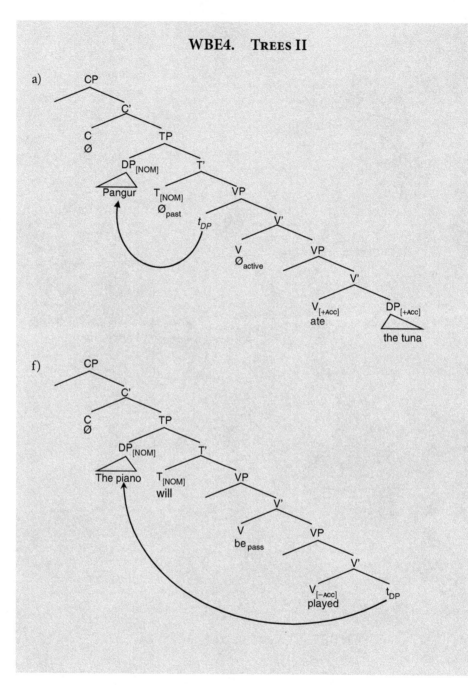

WBE4. Trees II

a)

f)

WBE5.   CASE

a) Heidi   nominative Case from T Ø*past*
    the airport   accusative Case from V *left*
    midnight   prepositional Case from P *at*
b) Jean   nominative Case from T *should*
    Ecuador   prepositional Case from P *to*
c) she   nominative Case from T Ø*pres*
    Damian   nominative Case from T *will*
    the mushrooms in chocolate sauce   accusative Case from V *ate*
    chocolate sauce   prepositional Case from P *in*
d) the book   nominative Case from T Ø*pres*
    French   prepositional Case from P *in*
e) Lionel   nominative Case from T Ø*pres*
    a book   accusative Case from V *written*
    French   prepositional Case from P *in*
f) Fiona   nominative Case from T Ø*pres*
    Theresa   prepositional Case from P *by*
g) the award   nominative Case from T Ø*past*
    the best presentation at the conference   prepositional Case from P *in*
    the conference   prepositional Case from P *at*
h) Morag   nominative Case from T Ø*past*
    the cheese   accusative Case from V *eaten*
i) the cheese   nominative Case from T Ø*past*
    the mouse   prepositional Case from P *by*

WBE6.   TREES III

b)

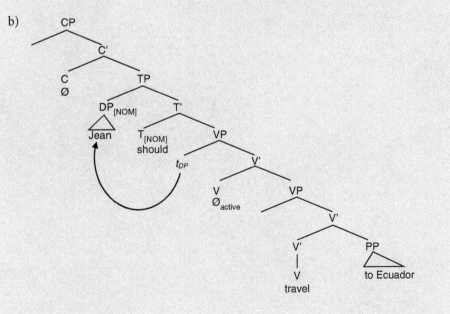

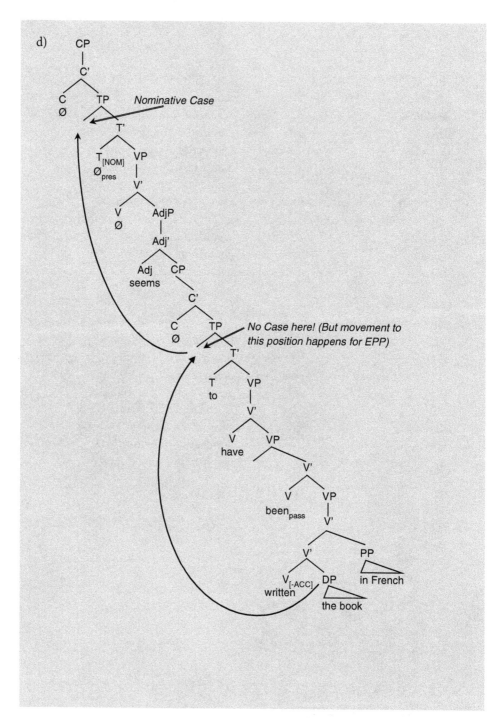

i)

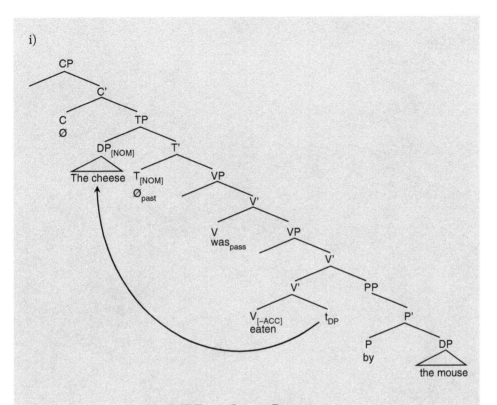

WBE7. IRISH PASSIVE

Part 1: The Irish passive does not use an auxiliary verb *be*. Instead, the verb raises through the voice position and takes on a special form in the passive. But more critically, the theme does not appear to become a subject. The theme retains its accusative Case. In English, no accusative Case is available for the theme, so it moves to subject position.

Part 2: We could claim that unlike English, the theta grid for the passive voice (which has to be a null auxiliary) does not require its complement to be [–ACC]. But then a different puzzle emerges: if the theme doesn't raise to subject position for nominative case, how is the EPP satisfied? One possibility is that the EPP is parameterized, and simply not present in Irish. This has in fact been claimed by the Irish linguist James McCloskey (1996). He points out that Irish generally lacks expletives in subject position, suggesting that the EPP is not active in the language.

Part 3:

a)

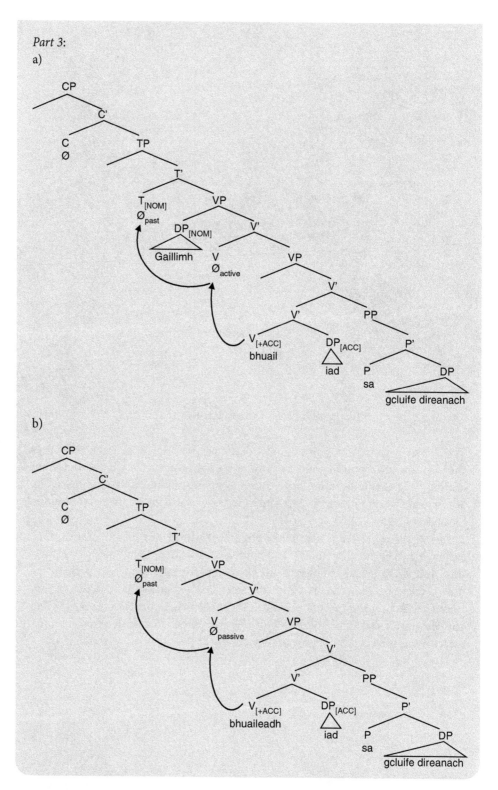

b)

chapter 12

Wh-movement and Locality Constraints

WORKBOOK EXERCISES

WBE1.   FIND THE GAP
[Data Analysis; Basic]

Each of the following sentences has a *wh*-phrase that has moved in it. Identify where in the sentence the *wh*-phrase starts.

a)   Which book were you reading?
b)   Who was sitting in the lobby?
c)   What has not been done?
d)   Who did Karen say Bob loved?
e)   What kind of ice-cream do you think Jimmy threw at the Santa in the mall?
f)   Where did you get that horrible lamp?
g)   Why did he eat the cardboard box?
h)   Why do you think he lost his underwear at the library?

The Syntax Workbook, First Edition. Andrew Carnie.
© 2013 Andrew Carnie. Published 2013 by John Wiley & Sons, Inc.

WBE2.   *Wh*-QUESTION TREES
[Data Analysis and Application of Skills; Basic]

Draw the trees for the sentences in WBE1.

WBE3.   *Wh*-QUESTIONS IN SCOTTISH GAELIC
[Data Analysis and Application of Skills; Advanced]

Draw the trees for the following sentences in Scottish Gaelic. Scottish Gaelic is like Irish in that it is a VSO language. (Data from Adger and Ramchand 2005.)

a) | Thuirt | sinn | gun | do-sgrìobh | i | an leabhar. |
    |--------|------|-----|------------|---|-------------|
    | say.PAST | we | that | PAST-write.PAST | she | the book |

"We said that she wrote the book."

b) | Dè | a | thuirt | sibh | a | sgrìobh | i? |
    |----|---|--------|------|---|---------|----|
    | what | WH-C | say.PAST | 2 S.POLITE | WH-C | write.PAST | she |

"What did you say that she wrote?"

WBE4.   RELATIVE CLAUSES I
[Data Analysis; Basic to Intermediate]

Each of the following sentences has a relative clause in it. Some have an overt *wh*-phrase which has moved, others do not. Identify where in the sentence the *wh*-phrase starts or where there is a missing element corresponding to the head noun.

a)   The car that I bought last week is already causing me problems.
b)   The person Heidi loves is leaving the country.
c)   The cell-phone, which came with an unlimited data plan, fell in the lake.
d)   The cat, who never finishes his breakfast, wants treats now.
e)   I can't remember the reason why I wanted to draw syntactic trees.

WBE5.   RELATIVE CLAUSES II
[Data Analysis and Application of Skills; Basic/Advanced]

Draw the trees for the sentences in WBE4.

WBE6.   RELATIVE CLAUSES IN SCOTTISH GAELIC
[Data Analysis and Application of Skills; Advanced]

Draw the tree for the following DP in Scottish Gaelic. (Data from MacAulay 1992.)

an	cù	a	bhìd	an	cat	a	mharbh an	luch
the	dog	WH-C	bite.PAST	the	cat	WH-C	kill.PAST the	mouse

"the dog that bit the cat that killed the mouse"

WBE7.   ISLANDS
[Application of Knowledge; Basic]

Each of the following sentences violates one of the constraints discussed in section 3 of the textbook. Identify which island constraint the following sentences violate.

a)   *What was that the cat ate disgusting?
b)   *Who do you both hate Jim and like?
c)   *What did you have the recollection that Fiona hates?
d)   *Who did you ask what he gave to?

WBE8.   HEAD-MOVEMENT AND NEGATION
[Application of Knowledge; Basic]

The grammaticality of the following sentence is surprising given the MLC. Explain why.

Fiona has not eaten her breakfast.

ANSWERS

WBE1.   FIND THE GAP

a)   Which book were you reading _____?
b)   Who _____ was sitting in the lobby?
c)   What _____ has not been done? (This one is a little tricky since it's a passive. The word *what* starts out as the object of *done*, but then moves to the subject position for Case, and then undergoes *wh*-movement. The underscore in (c) indicates the Case position of *what* (in the specifier of TP).
d)   Who did Karen say Bob loved _____?
e)   What kind of ice-cream do you think Jimmy threw _____ at the Santa in the mall?
f)   Where did you get that horrible lamp _____?
g)   Why did he eat the cardboard box ____?
h)   Why do you [$_{VP}$ think [$_{CP}$ he lost his underwear at the library] ____]? (This one is actually ambiguous: *why* could modify *think* or *lose* and be adjoined to either of those VPs. But the most likely interpretation is where it modifies *think*.)

WBE2.   *Wh*-QUESTION TREES

A note about the trees in this chapter: I've started regularly using triangles to abbreviate parts of the tree that aren't particularly relevant to the topic of the chapter. You should still avoid this where possible. Triangles are powerful and dangerous and should be left to the experts!

a)

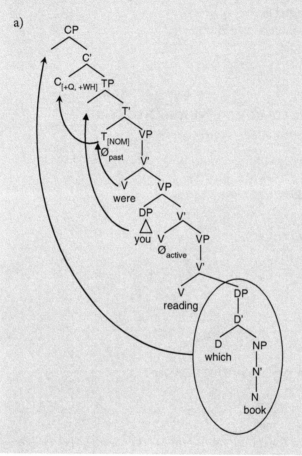

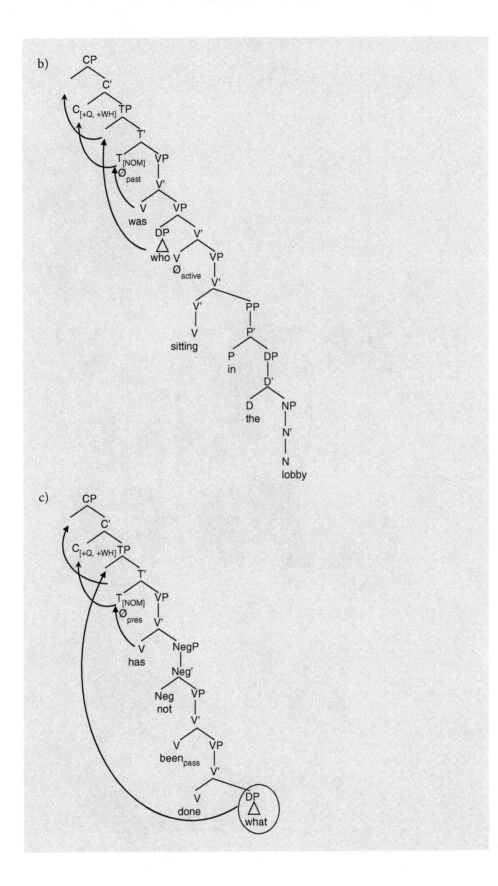

d)

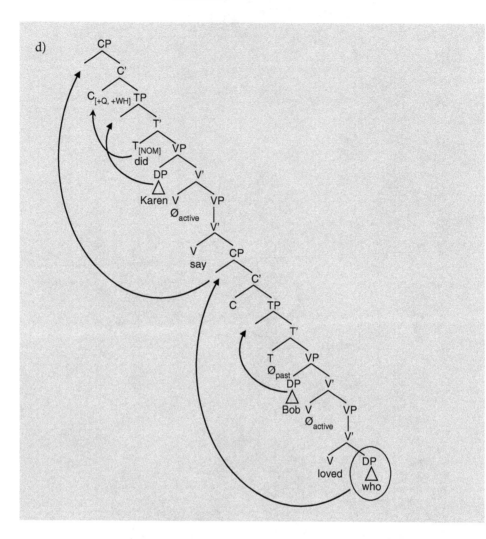

e)

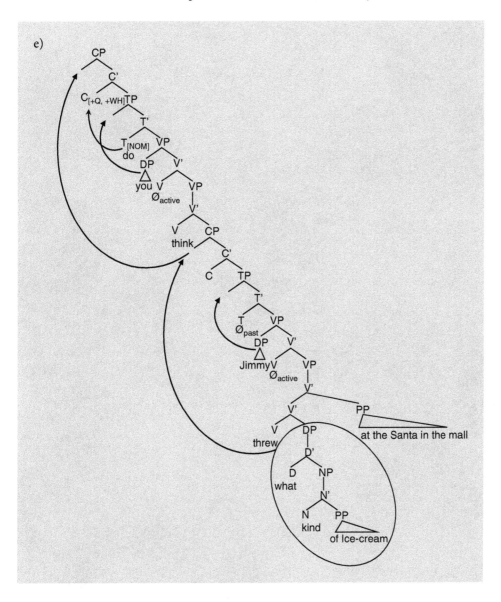

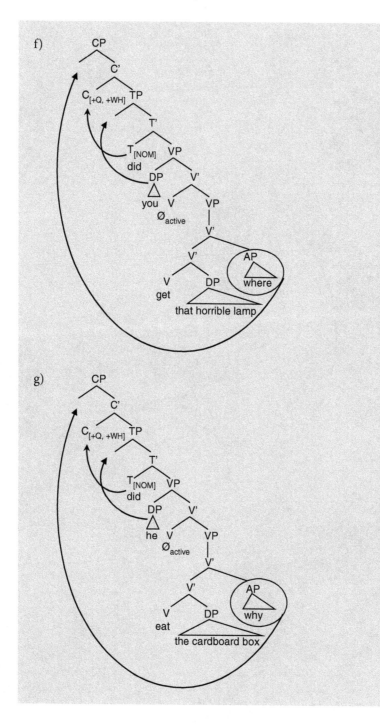

h)

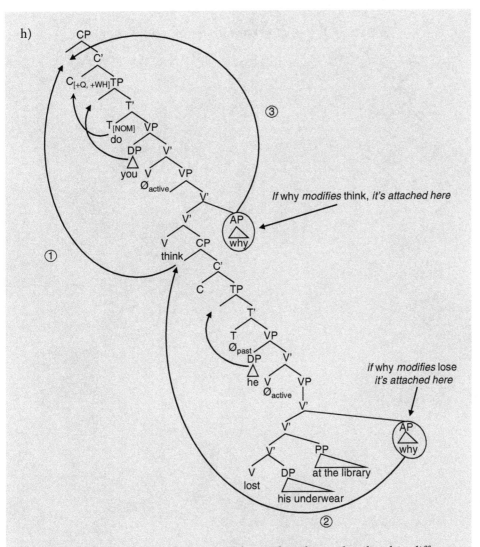

If *why* modifies think, *it's attached here*

if *why* modifies lose
it's attached here

Important note: I've combined two trees here. The *why* can be placed in different positions depending upon what it modifies. You *either* do movements ① and ② *or* you do ③. But you'd never combine all three movements together.

WBE3. *Wh*-QUESTIONS IN SCOTTISH GAELIC

a)

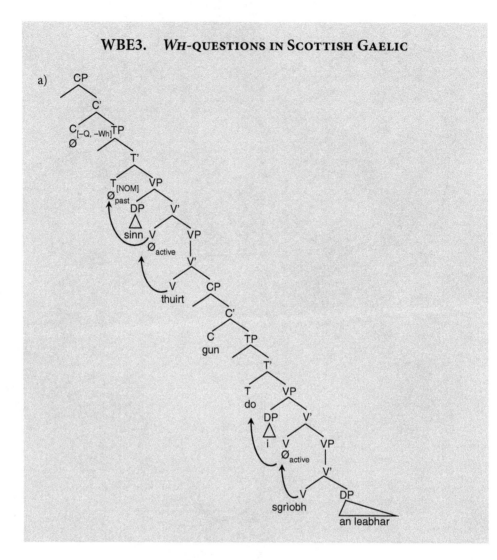

b)

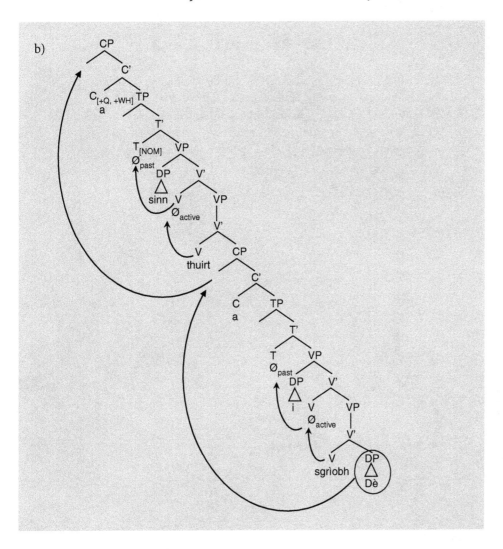

WBE4.   RELATIVE CLAUSES I

a)   The car that I bought _____ last week is already causing me problems.
b)   The person Heidi loves _____ is leaving the country.
c)   The cell-phone, which _____ came with an unlimited data plan, fell in the lake.
d)   The cat, who _____ never finishes his breakfast, wants treats now.
e)   I can't remember the reason why I wanted to draw syntactic trees _____.

WBE5.   RELATIVE CLAUSES II

a)

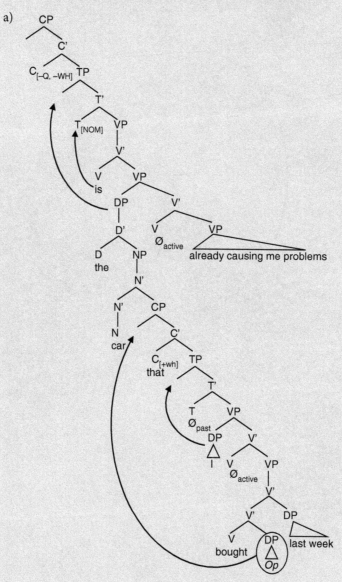

b)

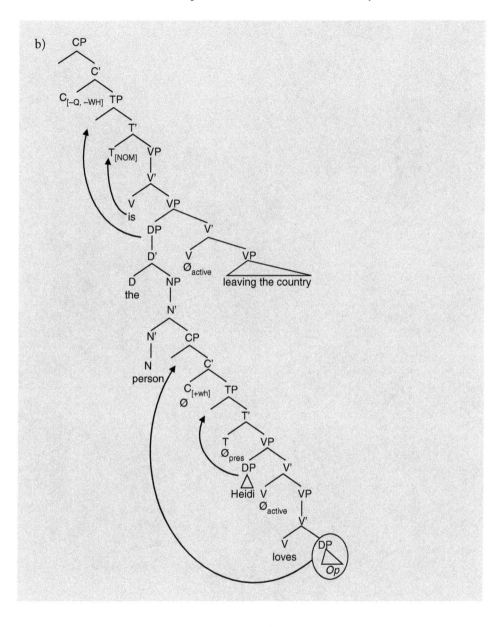

c)

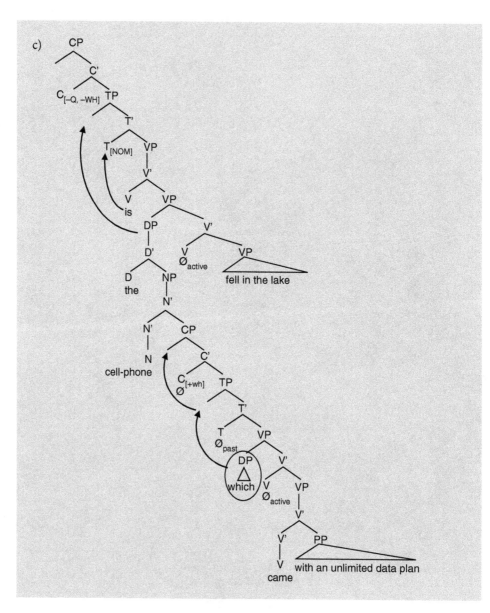

d)

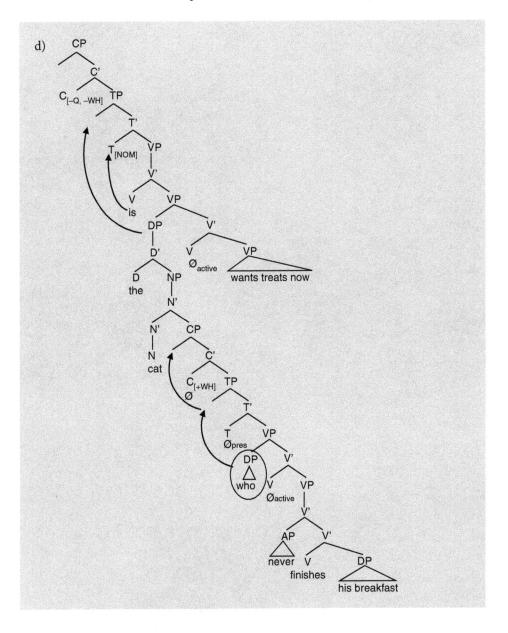

142 *Movement*

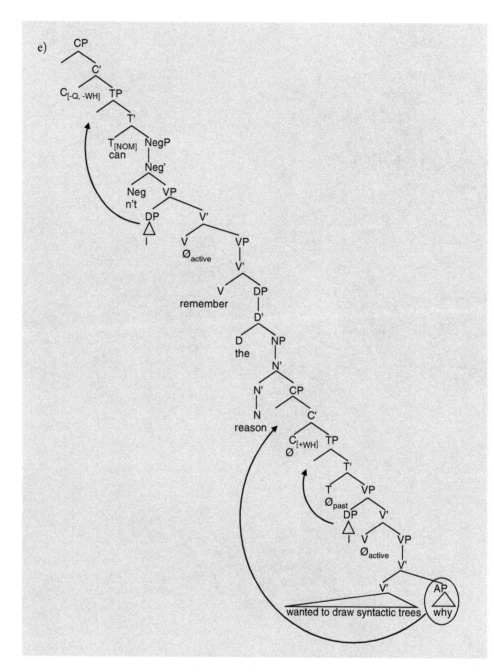

WBE6.   RELATIVE CLAUSES IN SCOTTISH GAELIC

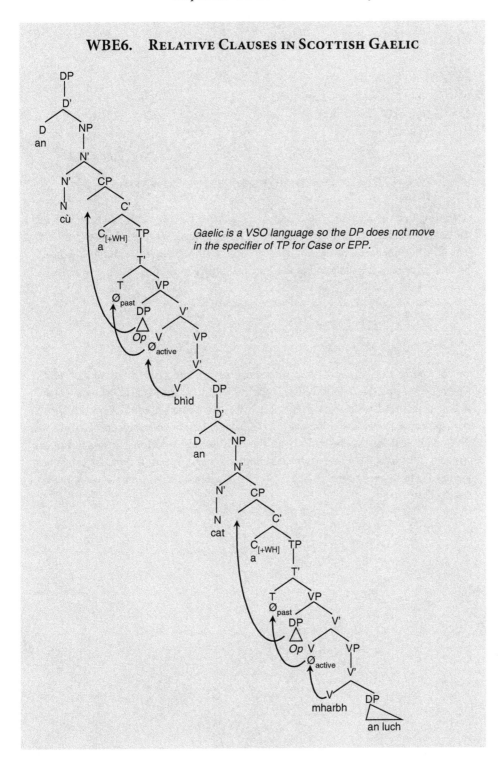

Gaelic is a VSO language so the DP does not move in the specifier of TP for Case or EPP.

WBE7.   ISLANDS

a)   Subject Condition
b)   Coordinate Structure Constraint
c)   Complex DP Constraint
d)   *Wh*-Island Constraint

WBE8.   HEAD-MOVEMENT AND NEGATION

Assuming that the auxiliary *has* has undergone V → T movement, as is standard for the highest auxiliary in English, it appears to have skipped over the negation head *not*. The head *not* occupies the closest head position to the starting position of the head. So this movement is a violation of the Minimal Link Condition.

[$_{TP}$ Fiona T [$_{NegP}$ not [$_{VP}$ has [$_{VP}$ eaten her breakfast]]]].

Closer head position

But of course this sentence is grammatical, contra the predictions of the MLC. There are two possible solutions to this contradiction: (1) the MLC is wrong or (2) *not* is not in the head position of NegP, but is instead either an adjunct on the VP or perhaps a specifier of NegP. Since the MLC makes a number of correct predictions we don't want to throw the baby out with the bath water. So option 1 is less desirable. Instead, 2 seems to be a better idea, although of course more data and investigation are needed to see if *not* behaves like a specifier or an adjunct. How might you go about testing that?

chapter 13

A Unified Theory of Movement

Workbook Exercises

WBE1. Bengali
[Data Analysis; Basic]

Based on the following data (from Bayer 2004), does Bengali have overt or covert *wh*-movement?

a) Ke   ešeche?
   who come.perf
   "Who has come?"

b) Tumi kake   dekhecho
   you   whom   saw
   "Who did you see?"

c) Tomar bondhu kɛno aše   mi?
   your   friend why   came   neg
   "Why did your friend not come?"

The Syntax Workbook, First Edition. Andrew Carnie.
© 2013 Andrew Carnie. Published 2013 by John Wiley & Sons, Inc.

WBE2. Vardar Macedonian, Mezquital Otomí, and Urim V → T

[Data Analysis; Basic]

Go back to the data in chapter 10, from WBE1 (Vardar Macedonian), WBE2 (Mezquital Otomí), and WBE3 (Urim) and determine if each of these has overt or covert V → T movement.

WBE3. Mezquital Otomí and Urim DP Movement

[Data Analysis; Basic]

Go back to the data in chapter 10, WBE2 (Mezquital Otomí) and WBE3 (Urim), and determine if each of these has overt or covert DP movement.

WBE4. Hungarian

[Data Analysis; Intermediate]

Consider the following data from Hungarian (data from Larson and Segal 1995).

a) János   többször   is   mindent   világosan   el   magyarázott.
   John   several   times   everything   clearly   PERF   explained
   "As for John on several occasions he explained everything clearly."

b) János   mindent   többször   is   világosan   el   magyarázott.
   John   everything   several   times   clearly   PERF   explained
   "As for John, everything was several times clearly explained by him."

Sentence (a) requires that *several times* has scope over *everything*. Sentence (b) only has the interpretation where *everything* has scope over *several times*. While not worrying about where the movement ends in Hungarian, explain how this data is evidence for overt Quantifier Raising.

Answers

WBE1. Bengali

Bengali has covert *wh*-movement.

WBE2. Vardar Macedonian, Mezquital Otomí, and Urim V → T

Vardar Macedonian has overt V → T movement; Mezquital Otomí has overt V → T movement; Urim has covert V → T movement.

WBE3.   Mezquital Otomí and Urim DP Movement

Mezquital Otomí is a VSO language so it has covert DP movement; Urim is trickier, since main verbs undergo covert V → T movement. Sentence (1) is a bit misleading. What is crucial in Urim is that subjects follow those tensed auxiliaries, so they are in the specifier of the VP. This tells us that it also has covert DP movement.

WBE4.   Hungarian

Scope in Hungarian is sensitive to linear order. In the (b) sentence the quantified DP appears before *többször is* "several times", suggesting it has moved there. This appears to be overt quantifier raising, which happens overtly in Hungarian.

chapter 14

Expanded VPs

WORKBOOK EXERCISES

WBE1. ENGLISH TREES
[Data Analysis; Basic/Advanced]

Draw the trees for the following sentences:

a)   The cat scratched the lady.
b)   The couch was destroyed.
c)   The waiter sent a free drink to the charming man.
d)   A free drink was sent to the charming man.
e)   The waiter sent the charming man a free drink.
f)   The charming man was sent a free drink.
g)   I asked the waiter if he ate the olives.

The Syntax Workbook, First Edition. Andrew Carnie.
© 2013 Andrew Carnie. Published 2013 by John Wiley & Sons, Inc.

WBE2. ENGLISH ADJACENCY
[Critical Thinking; Advanced]

In the chapter on X-bar theory, we claimed that the reason that direct objects had to be adjacent to the V was because they were complements to the V. In this chapter, however, we've claimed that both main verbs and objects move leftwards in English. But an explanation for the immediate adjacency of V and the accusative object can still be found with the tools we've proposed. Why must the object in English be immediately to the right of the verb? Illustrate with a tree. Further, why is this not the case in French?

ANSWERS

WBE1. ENGLISH TREES

a)

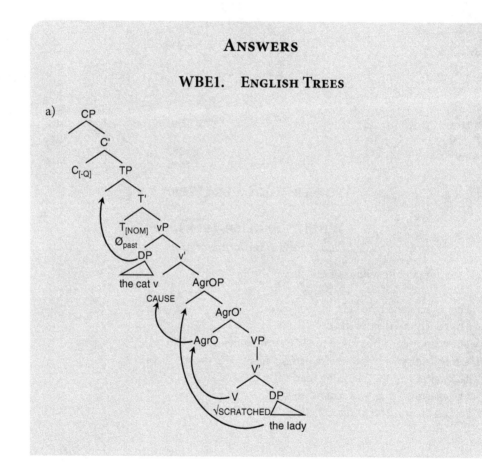

b)

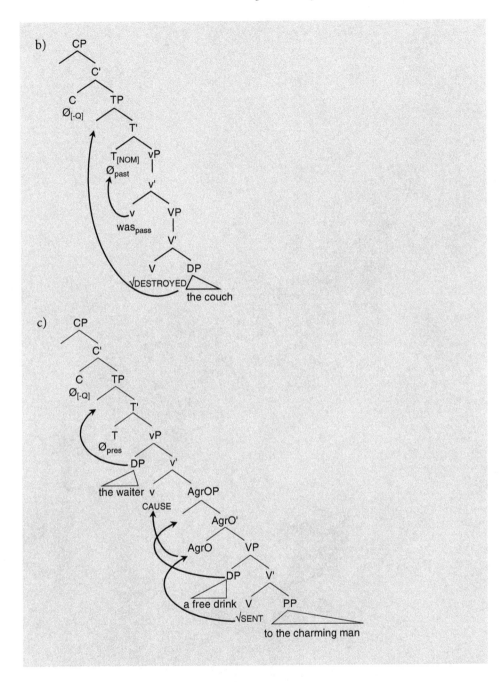

c)

154 *Advanced Topics*

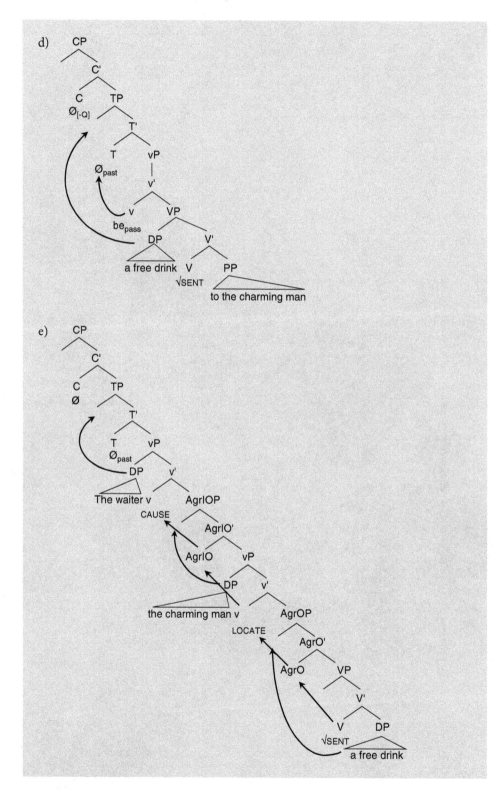

f)

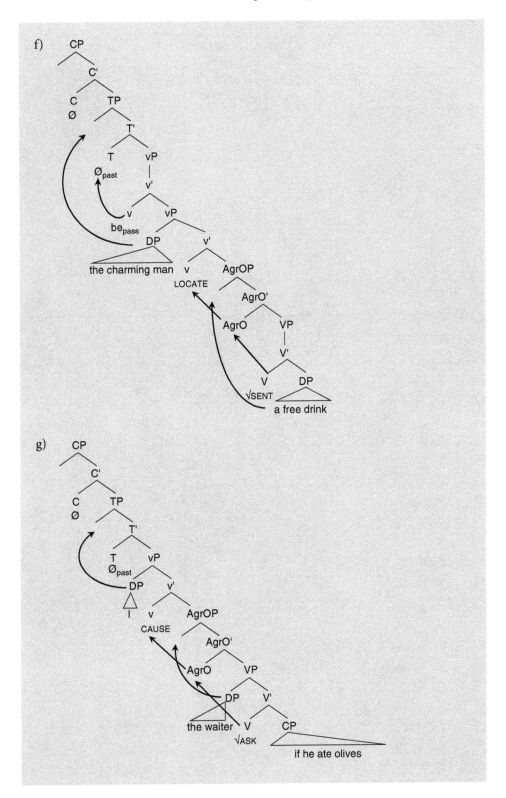

g)

WBE2.   ENGLISH ADJACENCY

The verb moves to the little v headed by CAUSE. The object moves to the specifier of AgrO and this position is immediately adjacent to the CAUSE head.

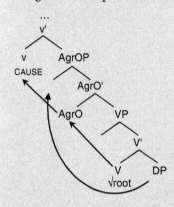

The reason that this doesn't happen in French is that the verb undergoes further movement to the T node.

part 4

Advanced Topics

chapter 15

Raising, Control, and Empty Categories

WORKBOOK EXERCISES[1]

WBE1. SUBJECT-TO-SUBJECT RAISING VS. SUBJECT CONTROL: IDIOMS
[Data Analysis; Basic]

Using the idiom test (e.g., *The shit is likely to hit the fan* vs. *#The shit is reluctant to hit the fan*), determine if the following are subject-to-subject raising or subject control constructions:

a) is bound   b) is able   c) is certain   d) is anxious

WBE2. IDIOM TEST: *IS READY*
[Data Analysis; Basic]

Does the predicate *is ready* behave like a control predicate or a raising predicate with respect to the idiom test?

---

[1] Some of the exercises in this unit are loosely based on those in Carnie (2011).

The Syntax Workbook, First Edition. Andrew Carnie.
© 2013 Andrew Carnie. Published 2013 by John Wiley & Sons, Inc.

WBE3.   SUBJECT-TO-SUBJECT RAISING VS. SUBJECT CONTROL: CLAUSAL SUBJECTS
[Data Analysis; Basic]

Using the clausal subject test (e.g., *That Jean likes candy is likely* vs. **That Jean likes candy is reluctant*), determine if the following are subject-to-subject raising or subject control constructions. For *is bound* use *is bound to be the case* instead of plain old *is bound*.

a)   is bound   b)   is able   c)   is certain   d)   is anxious

WBE4.   CLAUSAL SUBJECT TEST: *IS READY*
[Data Analysis; Basic]

Does the predicate *is ready* behave like a control predicate or a raising predicate with respect to the clausal subject test? Is this consistent with your result in WBE2?

WBE5.   SUBJECT-TO-SUBJECT RAISING VS. SUBJECT CONTROL: EXPLETIVE SUBJECTS
[Data Analysis; Basic]

Using the expletive subject/extraposition test (e.g., *It is likely that Jean likes candy* vs. **It is reluctant that Jean likes candy*), determine if the following are subject-to-subject raising or subject control constructions. For *is bound* use *is bound to be the case* instead of plain old *is bound*.

a)   is bound   b)   is able   c)   is certain   d)   is anxious

WBE6.   EXPLETIVE SUBJECT TEST: *IS READY*
[Critical Thinking; Challenging]

Does the predicate *is ready* behave like a control predicate or a raising predicate with respect to the expletive subject test? Is this consistent with your results in WBE2 and WBE4? What do we make of the contradiction between the tests here?

WBE7.   TREES I: SUBJECT-TO-SUBJECT RAISING AND SUBJECT CONTROL
[Application of Skills; Intermediate]

Draw the trees for the following sentences:

a)   Jean is able to eat candy on Fridays.
b)   Jean is certain to eat candy on Fridays.

WBE8.   SUBJECT-TO-OBJECT RAISING VS. OBJECT CONTROL: IDIOMS
[Data Analysis; Basic]

Using the idiom test (e.g., *Jean wants the shit to hit the fan* vs. *#Jean persuaded the shit to hit the fan*), determine if the following are subject-to-object raising or subject control constructions. For *consider, report,* and *believe* you'll have to use an embedded clause that's in the perfect (*the shit to have hit the fan*).

a) urge   b) consider   c) intend   d) report   e) believe   f) tell   g) has known

WBE9.   SUBJECT-TO-OBJECT RAISING VS. OBJECT CONTROL: ENTAILMENT
[Data Analysis; Intermediate/Advanced]

When one sentence logically requires that another sentence is true, we say the first sentence *entails* the second. The symbol we use for entails is ⊨. The symbol that we use to say that one sentence does not entail another is ⊭. When we have an object control sentence, the sentence as a whole entails that the object participates in the main verb action:

1)   Susan persuaded Bill to eat beef waffles ⊨ Susan persuaded Bill

With subject-to-object raising constructions this is not true. The whole sentence does not entail that the object participates in the main verb action:

2)   Susan wanted Bill to eat beef waffles ⊭ Susan wanted Bill

Using entailment judgments as a guide try to determine if the following predicates are subject-to-object raising or object control predicates. Sometimes you'll need to be creative with which predicates you put under these verbs. For example, the predicates *consider* and *report* use a non-finite clause like *Bill to be foolish*. With other verbs a more active predicate is required, so for these use *Bill to eat beef waffles*.

a) urge   b) consider   c) intend   d) report   e) believe   f) tell   g) has known

WBE10.   TREES II: SUBJECT-TO-OBJECT RAISING AND OBJECT CONTROL
[Application of Skills; Intermediate]

Draw the trees for the following sentences:

a)   Jean urged Fiona to eat candy on Fridays.
b)   Jean has known Fiona to eat candy on Fridays.

WBE11.   Subject-to-Object Raising in KiSwahili and Niuean
[Data Analysis; Advanced]

In the textbook, we argued that English sentences like *I want Bill to leave* involve raising the subject of the embedded clause up into the accusative Case position (the specifier of AgrOP), hence the name "subject-to-object" raising. In the early 1980s, Chomsky proposed a different analysis of these facts. He suggested that the subject of the embedded clause stayed in the specifier of TP, and that the main clause verb assigned accusative Case to it through something called **government**. This analysis, diagrammed in (a), was called **exceptional Case marking** or ECM.

a)

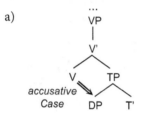

The complete details of ECM are not critical here. For the purpose of this question what is important is that in the ECM analysis, the subject of the embedded clause does not move into the main clause. Now consider the following data[2] from KiSwahili and Niuean. The (a) sentences are normal sentences. The (b) sentences have something like subject-to-object raising going on in them. Do these data support the subject-to-object raising analysis or the ECM analysis? Be precise about how the data supports one analysis and not the other.

1) a) | Ali | anaamini | yakama | mti | huu | unatosha | *KiSwahili* |
   |-----|----------|--------|-----|-----|----------|-------------|
   | Ali | believes | that | this | tree | suitable | |

   "Ali believes this tree is suitable."
   b) Ali anaamini mti huu yakama unatosha

2) a) | To | nakai | toka | e | au | ke | kai | he | pusi | e ika | *Niuean* |
   |----|-------|------|-----|-----|-----|-----|-----|------|--------|-----------|
   | FUT | not | let | the | I | that | eat | the | cat | the fish | |

   "I will not let the cat eat the fish."
   b) To nakai toka e au e pusi ke kai e ika.

---

[2]   I have been unable to track down the original source for this KiSwahili data, which I found in a problem set that I was given as a student. If you know what the source of this data is please let me know. The Niuean data is from Seiter (1980).

WBE12.   SUBJECT VS. OBJECT CONTROL: JUDGMENTS
[Data Analysis; Basic]

Determine for each of the following verbs who is doing the buying. Is it Michael or Josh?

a)   Michael promised Josh to buy a box of cereal.
b)   Michael persuaded Josh to buy a box of cereal.
c)   Michael ordered Josh to buy a box of cereal.
d)   Michael forced Josh to buy a box of cereal.

WBE13.   SUBJECT VS. OBJECT CONTROL
[Data Analysis; Basic]

For each of the following verbs, determine whether it is subject control, object control, or either.

a)   urge   b)   force   c)   intend   d)   requested   e)   tell   f)   consent   g)   hope

ANSWERS

WBE1.   SUBJECT-TO-SUBJECT RAISING VS. SUBJECT CONTROL: IDIOMS

a)   raising: *The shit is bound to hit the fan.*
b)   control: *#The shit is able to hit the fan.*
c)   raising: *The shit is certain to hit the fan.*
d)   control: *#The shit is anxious to hit the fan.*

WBE2.   IDIOM TEST: *IS READY*

For many native speakers the sentence ?*The shit is ready to hit the fan* is at least marginally acceptable with the idiomatic reading, which would lend itself to a raising analysis. However, try WBE4 and WBE6 as well to see if you get the same results.

WBE3.   SUBJECT-TO-SUBJECT RAISING VS. SUBJECT CONTROL: CLAUSAL SUBJECTS

a)   raising: *[That Bill likes beef-waffles] is bound to be the case.*
b)   control: **[That Bill likes beef-waffles] is able.*
c)   raising: *[That Bill likes beef-waffles] is certain.*
d)   control: **[That Bill likes beef-waffles] is anxious.*

WBE4.   CLAUSAL SUBJECT TEST: *IS READY*

Unlike the idiom test, the clausal subject test suggests that *is ready* is a control predicate. Clausal subjects are disallowed: **[That Bill likes beef-waffles] is ready.* You should note, however, that there are many exceptions to the clausal subject test. The verb *seems* disallows it, but shows all the other properties of raising.

WBE5.   SUBJECT-TO-SUBJECT RAISING VS. SUBJECT CONTROL: EXPLETIVE SUBJECTS

a)   raising: *It is bound to be the case that Bill likes beef waffles.*
b)   control: **It is able that Bill likes beef-waffles.*
c)   raising: *It is certain that Bill likes beef-waffles.*
d)   control: **It is anxious that Bill likes beef-waffles.* (This sentence is acceptable, but not with a expletive reading on the pronoun, only with a reading where there actually is something that is anxious.)

WBE6.   EXPLETIVE SUBJECT TEST: *IS READY*

The expletive subject (extraposition) test suggests that *is ready* is a control predicate: **It is ready that Bill likes beef-waffles.* This is consistent with the clausal subject test, but inconsistent with the idiom test. Note, however, that the predicate *is ready* in *The shit is ready to hit the fan* means something quite different from *is ready* in a sentence like *The contract is ready to be signed* or the more active *Bill is ready to eat beef-waffles.* In these latter two sentences, *is ready* means something like "is prepared for" but in *The shit is ready to hit the fan*, there's no sense of preparation, for me at least. I think this means that there are really two predicates *is ready*. One is a control predicate and means "is prepared for", and the other is a raising predicate and means "about to". For an interesting discussion of the raising vs. control status of *is ready*, see Faraci's (1974) Ph.D. dissertation.

WBE7. TREES I: SUBJECT-TO-SUBJECT RAISING AND SUBJECT CONTROL

a)

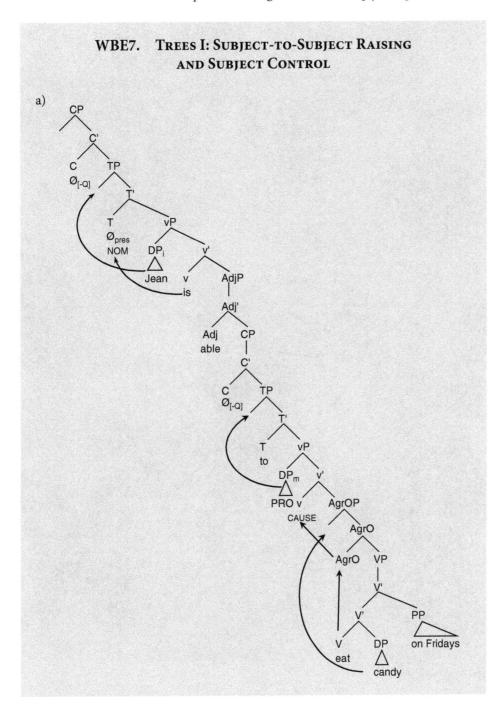

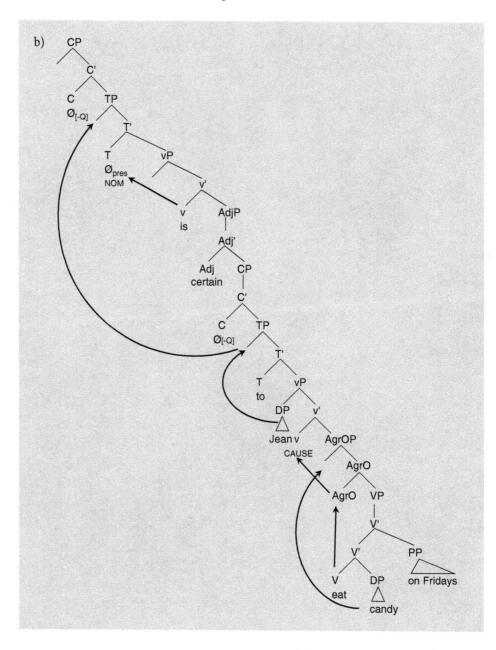

WBE8.   SUBJECT-TO-OBJECT RAISING VS. OBJECT CONTROL: IDIOMS

a)   control: *#I urged the shit to hit the fan.*
b)   raising: *I consider the shit to have hit the fan.*
c)   raising: *I intended the shit to hit the fan.*
d)   raising: *I reported the shit to have hit the fan.*
e)   raising: *I believe the shit to have hit the fan.*
f)   control: *#I told the shit to hit the fan.*
g)   raising: *I have known the shit to hit the fan.*

WBE9.   SUBJECT-TO-OBJECT RAISING VS. OBJECT CONTROL: ENTAILMENT

a)   control: *Sally urged Bill to eat beef waffles* ⊨ Sally urged Bill
b)   raising: *Sally considers Bill to be foolish* ⊭ Sally considers Bill
c)   raising: *Sally intended Bill to eat the beef waffle* ⊭ Sally intended Bill
d)   raising: *Sally reported Bill to be foolish* ⊭ Sally reported Bill
e)   raising: *Sally believed Bill to be foolish* ⊭ Sally believed Bill
f)   control: Sally *told Bill to eat beef waffles* ⊨ Sally told Bill
g)   raising: Sally *has known Bill to eat beef waffles* ⊭ Sally has known Bill

WBE10.   TREES II: SUBJECT-TO-OBJECT RAISING AND OBJECT CONTROL

a)

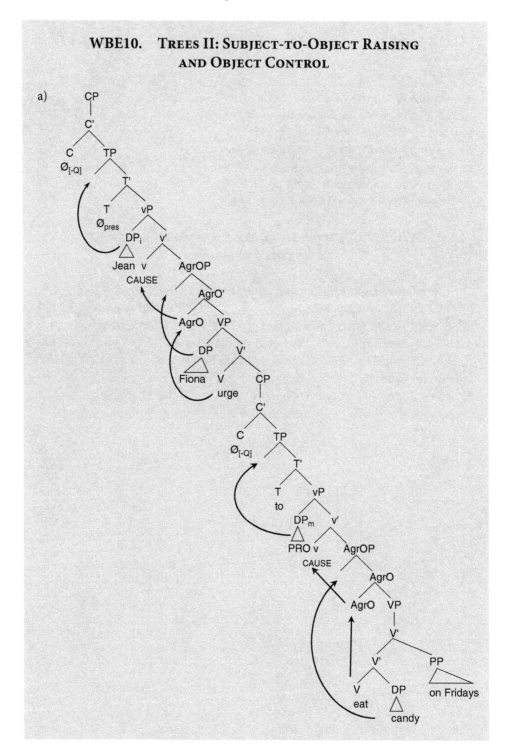

b)

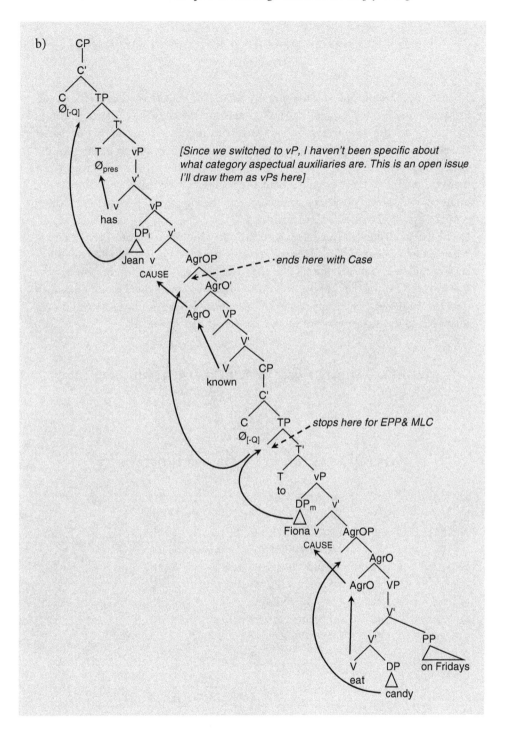

[Since we switched to vP, I haven't been specific about what category aspectual auxiliaries are. This is an open issue I'll draw them as vPs here]

WBE11.   Subject-to-Object Raising in KiSwahili and Niuean

The data in KiSwahili and Niuean point to a subject-to-object raising analysis over an ECM analysis. In the KiSwahili (1b), the subject of the embedded clause, *mti huu*, appears before the complementizer *yakama*. This means it is in the higher clause. Niuean is a VSO language, so the verb marks the left edge of the clause. In (2b) the subject *e pusi* appears to the left of the verb, so it too must be in the main clause. What is critical in both of these examples is that the subject of the embedded clause is not in the normal subject position for the language, showing that it is raised rather than getting Case via exceptional Case marking.

The KiSwahili and Niuean data raise other issues, however – problems that I don't know the solution to. You'll note that in both languages there is apparently no difference in finiteness between the (a) and the (b) sentences. In English, of course, subject-to-object raising only applies in non-finite clauses, where there is no nominative Case for the subject. There appears to be a nominative Case for the subject in the (a) sentences, so it's unclear why the subject raises in the (b) sentences.

WBE12.   Subject vs. Object Control: Judgments

a)   M   b) J   c) J   d) J

WBE13.   Subject vs. Object Control

a)	*urge*	OC	*I urged Bill to leave.*
b)	*force*	OC	*I forced Bill to leave.*
c)	*intend*	either	*I intended to leave.* (SC)
		or	*I intended Bill to be the winner.* (OC)
d)	*requested*	either	*I requested to leave.* (SC)
		or	*I requested Bill to leave.* (OC)
e)	*tell*	OC	*I told Bill to leave.*
f)	*consent*	SC	*I consented to leave.*
g)	*hope*	SC	*I hoped to leave.*

chapter 16

Ellipsis

WORKBOOK EXERCISES

WBE1.   HEBREW RESPONSIVE ELLIPSIS
AND SWAHILI VP ELLIPSIS

[Data Analysis and Creative Thinking; Basic]

Part 1: Hebrew is one of many languages where a common way to answer *yes* or *no* to a question is to repeat part of the clause back in either a positive or negative form. The analysis of this phenomenon typically holds that it is a kind of ellipsis similar to the English responses in (1):

1) Q.   Did Trixie find the toilet paper?
    A.   She did.

In the answer in (1), it appears as if the VP [*find the toilet paper*] has been elided under identity with the VP in the question. Consider now a similar question/answer pair in Hebrew (data from Goldberg 2005):

2) Q.   Šalaxt   etmol   et   ha-yeladim   le-beithasefer?
        send.you   yesterday   ACC   the-children   to-school
        "Did you send the children to school yesterday?"

The Syntax Workbook, First Edition. Andrew Carnie.
© 2013 Andrew Carnie. Published 2013 by John Wiley & Sons, Inc.

A.   Šalaxti
     send.1s
     "Yes" (literally "I sent").

The ellipsis data in (2) can be used to construct an argument that Hebrew has overt V → T movement. Construct such an argument.

Part 2: Now consider the following data from VP ellipsis in KiSwahili (data from Ngonyani 1996). Does KiSwahili have overt or covert V → T raising? Assume that the phrase *[kumnunulia motto viatu]* is a CP inside of a VP complement to *alitaka*.

3)   Mama   alitaka   kumnunulia   motto   viatu   na   baba   alitaka   pia.
     mother want   buy.inf   child   shoe   and   father want   also
     "Mother wanted to buy the child shoes and father did too" (literally "father wanted also").

WBE2.   Types of Ellipsis
[Data Analysis; Basic]

Identify the type of ellipsis (VP Ellipsis, Antecedent-Contained Deletion, Pseudogapping, or Sluicing) found in each of the following sentences. Also, identify the function word that licenses the ellipsis.

a)   My sister ate some food that I didn't.
b)   I think I put the money in one of these books, but I can't remember which.
c)   I've eaten more tacos in my life than I have burritos.
d)   John always said he would like to go to France but he still hasn't.

WBE3.   Quantifier Scope Parallelism in Ellipsis[1]
[Critical Thinking; Advanced]

Recall our discussion in chapter 13 of sentences like (1a). This sentence is ambiguous: it can mean either (1b) or (1c). The interpretation in (1b) is due to a covert operation of QR that puts the existentially quantified DP in a position where it c-commands (i.e. has scope) over the universal quantifier. We encoded this as movement of the quantified DP to the specifier of CP:

1)   a)   Every student read some paper.
     b)   *paraphrase 1*: There is some paper such that every student read it.
     c)   *paraphrase 2*: For each student, there is some paper (possibly a different one for each student), such that the student read it.
     d) $[_{CP}$ [some paper]$_i$ $[_{TP}$ every student [read t$_i$]

It's been observed that once you start combining QR and ellipsis an interesting effect emerges: the scopal interpretation of the clause with the elided VP has to be the same as the scopal

---

[1]   The idea for this problem set is based on discussion in Lasnik (2010). The original observations about scope effects in ellipsis constructions go back to Sag (1976), but the critical facts are discussed at length in Fox (1995).

interpretation of the antecedent clause. To see this at work look at (2). Sentence (2a) is identical to (1a), both in syntax and in meaning, except I've replaced *student* with *professor*:

2) a) Every professor read some paper.
    b) *paraphrase 1*: There is some paper such that every professor read it.
    c) *paraphrase 2*: For each professor, there is some paper (possibly a different one for each professor), such that the professor read it.
    d) [$_{CP}$ [some paper]$_i$ [$_{TP}$ every professor [read t$_i$]]

Now look at (3). This sentence has two conjoined clauses each with two quantifiers (although one of the quantifiers in the second clause has been elided via VP ellipsis). In principle each clause should allow both of the two readings, giving a total of four interpretations: (1b) + (2b), (1c) + (2c), (1b) + (2c), and (1c) + (2b). Interestingly, only the first two interpretations are available, (3b) and (3c). These are the ones in which there is a strict parallelism in interpretation between the clauses. The other two readings, (3d) and (3e), are totally unavailable and bizarre, even though they should be, in principle, available. The unavailable readings involve cases where the two conjuncts differ in whether or not they have had QR of the existential quantifier (i.e., in one of the two conjuncts (1d) or (2d) it has applied but in the other it has not).

3) a) Every student read some paper and every professor did too.
    b) *paraphrase 1*: There is some paper such that every student read it and every professor read it (1b + 2b).
    c) *paraphrase 2*: For each professor and each student, there is some paper (possibly a different paper for each professor and each student), such that the professor or student read it (1c + 2c).
    d) *impossible paraphrase 1*: *There is some paper such that every student read it, and for each professor there is a paper (possibly a different one for each professor), such that the professor read it.
    e) *impossible paraphrase 2*: *For each student, there is a paper (possibly a different one for each student) such that the student read it and there is some one paper such that every professor read that one paper.

With these data about the parallelism requirement of QR in mind, construct an argument in favor of an LF-copying analysis of ellipsis. Be explicit about what is copied and about why the parallelism requirement must hold. I'd also recommend writing a few sentences about how a PF-deletion account can't explain this requirement.

WBE4. ISLAND CONSTRAINT VIOLATIONS IN SLUICING
[Critical and Creative Thinking; Advanced]

In the textbook we noted that *wh*-movement out of a VP ellipsis site obeys island constraints contained within the ellipsis. Haj Ross observed in the 1960s that this isn't true for sluicing. *Wh*-movement in sluicing seems to violate island constraints without consequence (or with only very mild reduction in native speaker acceptability (examples from Ross 1969).

1) a) *I believe the claim that he bit someone but they don't know who I believe the claim that he bit (Complex DP Constraint violation).

   b) I believe the claim that he bit someone but they don't know who.

Does this fact serve as evidence for an LF-copying or PF-deletion account of sluices?

ANSWERS

WBE1. HEBREW RESPONSIVE ELLIPSIS AND SWAHILI VP ELLIPSIS

Part 1: In English, when we do responsive ellipsis, we only ever see a tensed auxiliary after the subject (e.g., *I did*), and never a main verb. English has covert V→T movement, so the verb doesn't move out of the VP before SPELLOUT. As a consequence the main verb in English always disappears when VP ellipsis occurs. By contrast, in Hebrew, the tensed main verb is used in responsive ellipsis, and the tensed main verb survives ellipsis. This means the verb raises out of the VP overtly (overt V→T movement) and thus survives responsive ellipsis.

Part 2: The facts of KiSwahili are very similar to those of Hebrew, except this is normal VP ellipsis rather than responsive ellipsis. What is surprising about KiSwahili is that the tensed main verb survives ellipsis. This shows that KiSwahili has overt V→T movement, where the V is no longer inside the VP.

WBE2. TYPES OF ELLIPSIS

a) ACD: *didn't*.
b) Sluicing: *which*.
c) Pseudogapping (comparative subdeletion): *have*.
d) VP ellipsis: *hasn't*.

WBE3. QUANTIFIER SCOPE PARALLELISM IN ELLIPSIS

In the discussion of the differences between the two hypotheses, we claimed that one difference between LF copying and PF deletion is that in PF deletion, the two VPs have independent structures before SPELLOUT and at LF. In the LF-copying analysis, by contrast, the second VP gets its LF by having the VP in the first clause copied over.

The scope parallelism requirement on VP ellipsis suggests that the latter hypothesis is correct. Since the two clauses must have identical or parallel scope interpretations, this follows naturally from the view that the first VP is simply copied over to the second. (More precisely, If QR has applied, then the VP with the trace gets copied into the second clause and the second VP is interpreted as if the existential quantifier has wide scope. If QR has not applied, the VP with the existential in situ sits within the scope of the subject of the second clause.) The PF-deletion hypothesis makes the wrong predictions. Since each VP has its own life independent of the other, there's no particular reason that the two VPs should have identical LFs, so all four possible interpretations are predicted.

WBE4.   ISLAND CONSTRAINT VIOLATIONS IN SLUICING

The fact that sluices don't seem to obey island conditions is expected if the LF-copying theory is correct and the elided TP is just a pro-form without any structure. If there's no structure in the TP, then there are no islands within it to violate. This would support the LF-copying theory. On the other hand, VP ellipsis is sensitive to island constraints, so that supports PF deletion of VP structure. This conundrum (and related puzzles) is discussed at length in Merchant (2001) if you want to see how this kind of conflict might be resolved.

chapter 17

Advanced Topics in Binding Theory

WORKBOOK EXERCISES

WBE1.   PASSAMAQUODDY[1]
[Data Analysis and Creative Thinking; Intermediate]

Consider the following *wh*-questions from Passamaquoddy, an Algonquian language spoken in Maine and New Brunswick. Explain how this data supports the copy theory of movement.

a)   [$_{CP}$Tayuwe   [$_{TP}$kt-itomups   [$_{CP}$tayuwe   [$_{TP}$apc   k-tol-i
      when   2-say   when   again   2-there-go

malsanikuwam-ok]]]]?
store-LOC
"When did you say you're going to go to the store?"

b)   [$_{CP}$Wen   [$_{TP}$Mali   wewitahamacil   [$_{CP}$*wen* kisiniskamuk]]]?
      who   Mary   remember   who dance.with
      "Who does Mary remember I danced with?"

---

[1]   Data from Bruening (2006); glosses have been simplified.

The Syntax Workbook, First Edition. Andrew Carnie.
© 2013 Andrew Carnie. Published 2013 by John Wiley & Sons, Inc.

WBE2.   MOVEMENT AND BINDING[2]
[Data Analysis and Application of Skills; Intermediate]

Consider the following examples. Explain how the copy theory of movement accounts for the binding of the anaphors in these sentences.

a)   Morgan$_i$ seems to take care of himself$_i$.
b)   [Which athlete]$_i$ do you expect will outdo himself$_i$ in the race?

WBE3.   BINDING DOMAIN
[Data Analysis and Application of Skills; Basic]

Assume that *each other* is an anaphor. Identify the binding domain for each pronoun and anaphor in the following sentences:

a)   [Bill and Tim]$_i$ know [each other]$_i$.
b)   [Bill and Tim]$_i$ know [each other]$_i$'s mothers.
c)   *[Bill and Tim]$_i$ know [them]$_i$.
d)   [Bill and Tim]$_i$ love [their]$_i$ mothers.[3]
e)   *[Bill and Tim]$_i$ looked at [Mary's drawings of [each other]$_i$].
f)   [Bill and Tim]$_i$ looked at [Mary's drawings of [them]$_i$].
g)   [Bill and Tim]$_i$ thought that [[each other]$_i$ had brought the gift].

ANSWERS

WBE1.   PASSAMAQUODDY

In Passamaquoddy, we hear actual overt realization of the *wh*-trace in the intermediate CP specifier (*tayuwe* in (a) and *wen* in (b)).

WBE2.   MOVEMENT AND BINDING

a)   The trace of *Morgan* is the subject of the clause containing the anaphor. The covert copy of *Morgan* binds the anaphor.
b)   The covert trace of *which athlete* is in the same clause as the anaphor and binds it.

---

[2]   Thanks to Yosuke Sato for contributing this problem set.
[3]   This example has a lot of ambiguity in it. It could mean they each love their own mothers, or it could mean that they both love both of their mothers. We'll assume the latter reading here.

WBE3.   BINDING DOMAIN

a)   The CP.

b)   The CP. (The anaphor requires a potential subject, so the DP doesn't count.)

c)   The CP.

d)   The DP *[their mothers]*. (The pronoun does not require a potential subject, so the DP does count.)

e)   The DP *[Mary's drawings of [each other]$_i$]*. *Mary* is the potential antecedent.

f)   The DP *[Mary's drawings of [them]$_i$]*

g)   The main clause DP. *[Bill and Tim]$_i$* is the potential (and actual) antecedent.

chapter 18

Polysynthesis, Incorporation, and Non-configurationality

WORKBOOK EXERCISES

WBE1.   PSEUDOINCORPORATION
[Data Analysis and Creative Thinking; Intermediate]

There is a phenomenon common in many Polynesian languages called **pseudoincorporation** or **juxtaposition**. In pseudoincorporation, a verb and its complement behave like a single unit syntactically. Explain how the following data argues for a movement analysis. What you'll be using to construct this argument are "landmarks" around which elements seem to flip position. Negation and adverbs were two such landmarks when we were talking about the difference between French and English in chapter 10. Sentence (1) is from Samoan, and the relevant landmark is the subject *[ai e ia]*. Samoan is a VSO language. Sentence (2) is from Kusaein, and the relevant landmark is the adverb *upac* "diligently". The data is from Mithun (1984).

1) a)

Po	ʻo	āfea	e	tausi	**ai**	**e**	**ia**	*tama?*	*Samoan*
Q	PRED	when	TNS	care	**CL**	**ERG**	**he**	child?	

   "When does he take care of children?"

   b)

Po	ʻo	āfea	e	tausi	*tama*	**ai**	**e**	**ia?**
Q	PRED	when	TNS	care	child	**CL**	**ERG**	**he**

   "When does he take care of children?"

The Syntax Workbook, First Edition. Andrew Carnie.
© 2013 Andrew Carnie. Published 2013 by John Wiley & Sons, Inc.

2) a) Sah   el   twem   **upac**   *mitmit*   sac.   **Kusaein**
       sah   he   sharpen diligently knife   the
       "Sah is sharpening the knife diligently."

   b) Sah   el   twetwe   *mitmit*   **upac**.
       Sah   he   sharpen knife   diligently.
       "Sah is diligently knife-sharpening."

WBE2. GREENLANDIC
[Data Analysis; Basic]

Explain how the following sentence of Greenlandic Eskimo (data from Sadock 1991) serves as evidence for a movement approach to incorporation.

a) Kunngip   panippassuaqarpoq.
    king.POSS   daughter.many.have.INDIC.3S
    "There are many king's daughters."

WBE3. MAPADUNGUN AND MOHAWK DPs[1]
[Data Analysis and Critical Thinking; Intermediate]

Mapadungun (1) and Mohawk (2) are non-configurational languages. Recall from chapter 12 that adjuncts are islands for movement. Explain how the data below is evidence for a CLLD adjunct analysis of non-configurationality in Mapadungun and Mohawk.

1) a) Pe-fi-n   Maria   ñi   metawe.
       see-OBJ-1sS   Maria   POSS   vessel
       "I saw Maria's metawe."

   b) *Iney   pe-fi-mi   ñi   metawe?
       who   see-OBJ-2sS POSS   vessel
       "Who did you see the metawe of?"

2) *Úhka   wa'-te-she-noru'kwányu-'   ne raó-skare?
    who   fact-DUP-2sS/FsO-kiss-PUNC   ne MsP-Friend
    "Whose girlfriend did you kiss?"

Advanced additional question: Imagine that DPs were not adjuncts in these languages. What other constraint that we have proposed in the book would explain these data?

---

[1] Data from Baker (2006).

ANSWERS

WBE1. PSEUDOINCORPORATION

In a VSO language like Samoan, you can tell there has been V → T head movement because the verb appears to the left of the subject. In the pseudoincorporation sentence, the object also appears to the left of the subject – it could only appear in this position if it also underwent V → T movement. This means that it has to be part of the verb and thus incorporated. In SVO languages one of the ways we can tell a verb has undergone V → T movement is if adverbs appear between the verb and the direct object. In Kuseain pseudoincorporated sentences the adverb appears to the right of both the verb and the object. This suggests that the object has incorporated into the verb and then the V + N complex undergoes V → T. Of course this data is less conclusive than the Samoan, because adverbs are typically much looser in their ordering than subjects.

WBE2. GREENLANDIC

Part of the complex DP "many king's daughters" is incorporated into the V (the part that means "many … daughters" and part is not (the part that means "king's"). This constituent is broken up by the movement of the "many daughters" into the V, leaving "king's" as a remnant.

WBE3. MAPADUNGUN AND MOHAWK DPs

The ungrammaticality of *wh*-movement from within a DP follows directly if all DPs are adjuncts in non-configurational languages because adjuncts are islands and block *wh*-movement from within them. Of course, extraction from within DPs is, in general, disallowed due to the Complex DP Constraint. So in order for this argument to really hold water, we'd need to show that it isn't the DP itself that's blocking extraction in these cases, but rather that its adjunct status is the problem.

References

Note: This list only includes works directly cited in this workbook. However, the origins of the ideas discussed and examined in this work extend far beyond this list. See the reference list in the main textbook for a more comprehensive list of source material.

Adger, D. and G. Ramchand (2005) Merge and move: *Wh*-dependencies revisited. *Linguistic Inquiry* 36, 161–93.

Akmajian, A. and F. Heny (1975) *An Introduction to the Principles of Transformational Syntax.* MIT Press.

Aldai, G. (2009) Is Basque morphologically ergative? Western Basque vs. Eastern Basque. *Studies in Language* 33, 783–821.

Bacheller, I. (1903) *Darrel of the Blessed Isles.* Lothrop Publishing Co. http://www.gutenberg.org/files/12102/12102.txt.

Baker, M. C. (2006) On zero agreement and polysynthesis. In Peter Ackema, Patrick Brandt, Maaike Schoorlemmer, and Fred Weeman (eds.) *Arguments and Agreement.* Oxford University Press, pp. 289–320.

Bayer, J. (2004) *Wh-in-situ. Ms.* University of Konstanz. http://ling.uni-konstanz.de/pages/home/bayer/pdf/pdf/wh-in-situ.pdf.

Breen, G. and B. Blake (2007) *The Grammar of Yalarnnga: A Language of Western Queensland.* Pacific Linguistics, Research School of Pacific and Asian Studies, Australian National University.

Bruening, B. (2006) Differences between the *wh*-scope-marking and *wh*-copy constructions in Passamaquoddy. *Linguistic Inquiry* 37, 25–49.

Carnie, A. (2011) *Modern Syntax.* Cambridge University Press.

Chaughley, R. C. (1982) *The Syntax and Morphology of the Verb in Chepang.* Research School of Pacific Studies, Australian National University.

Comrie, B. (1973) The ergative: Variations on a theme. *Lingua* 32, 239–53.

Davies, W. (1981) *Choctaw Clause Structure.* Ph.D. dissertation, University of California San Diego.

Doron, E. and G. Khan (2011) PCC and ergative case: Evidence from Neo-Aramaic. Paper presented at the 29th West Coast Conference on Formal Linguistics, April 22, 2011, Tucson, Arizona.

Faraci, F. (1974) *Aspects of the Grammar of Infinitives and For-phrases.* Ph.D. dissertation, MIT.

Farrell, P. (1994) *Thematic Relations and Relational Grammar.* Garland.

Fox, D. (1995) Economy and scope. *Natural Language Semantics* 3, 283–341.

Fromkin, V. and R. Rodman (1978) *An Introduction to Language,* 2nd ed. Holt McDougal.

Goldberg, L. (2005) *Verb-Stranding VP Ellipsis: A Cross-Linguistic Study.* Ph.D. dissertation, McGill University.

The Syntax Workbook, First Edition. Andrew Carnie.
© 2013 Andrew Carnie. Published 2013 by John Wiley & Sons, Inc.

Grimshaw, J. (1990) *Argument Structure*. MIT Press.

Harris, A. (2011) The diachrony of Case patterns. Collitz Institute Lecture, LSA Summer Institute of Linguistics, July 19, 2011, Boulder, Colorado.

Jelinek, E. and R. Demers (1994) Predicates and pronominal arguments in Straits Salish. *Language* 70, 697–736.

Kester, E.-P. and P. Sleeman (2002) N-ellipsis in Spanish. *Linguistics in the Netherlands* 2002, pp. 107–16.

Larson, R. and G. Segal (1995) *Knowledge of Meaning: An Introduction to Semantic Theory*. MIT Press.

Lasnik, H. (2010) On ellipsis: Is material that is phonetically absent but semantically present present or absent syntactically? In H. Götzche (ed.) *Memory, Mind and Language*. Cambridge Scholars Publishing, pp. 221–42.

Lazarova-Nikovska, A. (2003) On interrogative sentences in Macedonian: A generative perspective. *Working Papers in English and Applied Linguistics* 9, 129–59. University of Cambridge, Research Centre for English and Applied Linguistics.

MacAulay, M. (1992) *The Celtic Languages*. Cambridge University Press.

McCloskey, J. (1996) Subjects and Subject Positions in Irish. In Robert Borsley and Ian Roberts (eds.) *The Syntax of the Celtic Languages: A Comparative Perspective*. Cambridge University Press, pp. 241–83.

Mchombo, S. (2004) *The Syntax of Chicheŵa*. Cambridge University Press.

Merchant, J. (2001) *The Syntax of Silence: Sluicing, Islands, and the Theory of Ellipsis*. Oxford University Press.

Merrifield, W. R., C. Naish, C. Rensch, and G. Story (2003) *Laboratory Manual for Morphology and Syntax*, 7th ed. Summer Institute of Linguistics.

Mithun, M. (1984) The evolution of noun incorporation. *Language* 60, 847–94.

Mithun, M. (1991) Active/agentive Case marking and its motivations. *Language* 67, 510–46.

Ngonyani, M. D. (1996) VP ellipsis in Ndendeule and Swahili applicatives. *Syntax at Sunset: UCLA Working Papers in Syntax and Semantics* 1, 109–28.

Payne, T. E. (1997) *Describing Morphosyntax: A Guide for Field Linguists*. Cambridge University Press.

Pinker, S. (1995) *The Language Instinct*. Harper Perennial.

Roeper, T. (1987) Implicit arguments and the head-complement relation. *Linguistic Inquiry* 18, 267–310.

Ross, J. R. (1969) Guess who? In R. Binnick, A. Davison, G. Green, and J. Morgan (eds.) *Papers from the Fifth Regional Meeting of the Chicago Linguistic Society, April 18–19, 1969*. Dept. of Linguistics, University of Chicago, pp. 252–86.

Sadock, J. (1991) *Autolexical Syntax: A Theory of Parallel Grammatical Representations*. University of Chicago Press.

Sag, I. (1976) *Deletion and Logical Form*. Ph.D. dissertation, MIT.

Seiter, W. J. (1980) *Studies in Niuean Syntax*. Garland.

Stenson, N. (1989) Irish autonomous impersonals. *Natural Language and Linguistic Theory* 7, 379–406.

Index

In the following index, the numbers given do not refer to page number but to chapter and exercise number. So for example 13:2 means chapter 13, WBE2. Exercises about English are not indexed under "English" but under the topic they refer to.

The Syntax Workbook, First Edition. Andrew Carnie.
© 2013 Andrew Carnie. Published 2013 by John Wiley & Sons, Inc.